Nathan Ti

 Nathan Tidridge was awarded the Queen's Golden Jubilee Medal for his ten years of volunteer support in the education of Canadians on the role of the Crown. He teaches Canadian history and government at Waterdown District High School and was awarded the Premier's Award for Teaching Excellence (Teacher of the Year) in 2008. In 2011, he received the Charles Baillie Award for Excellence in Secondary School Teaching from Queen's University.

On May 22, 2012, Nathan Tidridge was one of six Ontarians presented with a Diamond Jubilee Medal by His Royal Highness the Prince of Wales for exemplifying Her Majesty's 21st birthday pledge "I declare before you all that my whole life whether it be long or short shall be devoted to your service." The ceremony took place at Queen's Park in the presence of Her Royal Highness the Duchess of Cornwall and His Honour, the Lieutenant Governor of Ontario.

Nathan lives in Waterdown, Ontario, with his wife Christine and daughters Sophie and Elyse. His previous publications include *Canada's Constitutional Monarchy* (2012) and *Beyond Mainland* (2009). He maintains a website dedicated to educating Canadians about their constitutional monarchy at *www.canadiancrown.com*.

A QUEST BIOGRAPHY

PRINCE EDWARD, DUKE OF KENT

FATHER OF THE CANADIAN CROWN

NATHAN TIDRIDGE

DUNDURN
TORONTO

Editor: Jane Gibson
Copy Editor: Laura Harris
Design: Jesse Hooper and Jennifer Scott
Printer: Webcom

Library and Archives Canada Cataloguing in Publication

Tidridge, Nathan, 1978-
         Prince Edward, Duke of Kent : father of the Canadian Crown / Nathan Tidridge.

(A Quest biography)
Includes bibliographical references and index.
Issued also in electronic formats.
ISBN 978-1-4597-0789-4

1. Edward Augustus, Prince, Duke of Kent, 1767-1820. 2. Québec (Province)--History--1791-1841. I. Title. II. Series: Quest biography

DA506.A6T54 2013   941.073092   C2012-908625-8

1   2   3   4   5   17   16   15   14   13

We acknowledge the support of the Canada Council for the Arts and the Ontario Arts Council for our publishing program. We also acknowledge the financial support of the Government of Canada through the Canada Book Fund and Livres Canada Books, and the Government of Ontario through the Ontario Book Publishing Tax Credit and the Ontario Media Development Corporation.

Care has been taken to trace the ownership of copyright material used in this book. The author and the publisher welcome any information enabling them to rectify any references or credits in subsequent editions.

J. Kirk Howard, President

Printed and bound in Canada.

Visit us at
Dundurn.com | Definingcanada.ca | @dundurnpress | Facebook.com/dundurnpress

Dundurn
3 Church Street, Suite 500
Toronto, Ontario, Canada
M5E 1M2

Gazelle Book Services Limited
White Cross Mills
High Town, Lancaster, England
LA1 4XS

Dundurn
2250 Military Road
Tonawanda, NY
U.S.A. 14150

To Carl Draksler

Teacher, mentor, and friend.

I first met Mr. Draksler when I was a Grade 10 history student at Waterdown District High School and everyday Carl would demonstrate the inherent nobility of teaching. Now, nearly twenty years since sitting in his classroom, I am proud to be working in his department.

"Do not forget me."

— Prince Edward to his wife,
Princess Victoria of Saxe-Coburg-Saalfeld,
on his deathbed, 1820

Contents

Foreword

Residing in Canada during the formative period following the Royal Proclamation of 1763, the Duke of Kent participated in a society struggling to define itself. Prince Edward represented the vibrant role of the Crown in this country, and was the first to conceptually unite the English- and French-speaking peoples of British North America under the term "Canadian." When he travelled to the newly constituted province of Upper Canada in 1792, Prince Edward visited the Loyalist settlements, emphasizing British sovereignty in an area threatened by a growing American republic, a situation that would come to a head with the War of 1812. In Lower Canada, the Duke embodied the role of the crown as an encourager and protector of French culture on the continent. Appointed commander-in-chief of Nova Scotia and New Brunswick, and later for all of British North America, the Duke of Kent had a dramatic impact on the Maritimes. For Halifax, in particular, the Duke's time in residence is still considered a "Golden Age" by Haligonians.

Nathan Tidridge appropriately calls the Duke of Kent the "most honoured of Canada's forgotten historical figures," and this phrase rings true when I look out across my province. In Nova Scotia, and indeed in much of the rest of Canada, most notably Prince Edward Island, his name is still very much alive, a testimony to a man who lived with us longer than most of his notable contemporaries, and who now enjoys pride of place in our history books.

Interestingly, Tidridge refers to the Duke of Kent as the "Father of the Canadian Crown." Indeed, it was the Duke of Kent who began the process of meaningful travel throughout Canada, a hallmark of Canada's Royal family today. The Duke's presence in the country embodied the complex constitution developing in British North America, as well as the Crown's relationships with First Nations, French Canada, Loyalist settlements, and even the United States. Finally, it is the Duke's only child, Queen Victoria, who presided over Confederation and the creation of the Dominion of Canada.

As Her Majesty's representative in the province of Nova Scotia, I am pleased that this work highlights the place of Prince Edward in our national story.

Brigadier-General The Hon. J.J. Grant, CMM, ONS, CD (Ret'd)
Lieutenant Governor of Nova Scotia

Courtesy of the Office of the Lieutenant Governor of Nova Scotia.

Portrait of His Honour Brigadier-General The Honourable J.J. Grant, CMM, ONS, CD, Lieutenant Governor of Nova Scotia.

Acknowledgements

Writing a book creates a community that surrounds its text, and I am honoured by the one encompassing *Prince Edward, Duke of Kent: Father of the Canadian Crown*. As a loyal Friend of the Canadian Crown, it is my hope that this book brings to light an extraordinary story of our constitutional monarchy.

It was historian and author Arthur Bousfield of the Canadian Royal Heritage Trust who first told me about Prince Edward Augustus, Duke of Kent. This book would not exist without Arthur's championship of the Duke as one of Canada's important historic figures.

For granting access to the invaluable Royal Archives, including the personal diaries of Queen Victoria, I would like to express my sincere appreciation to Her Majesty Queen Elizabeth II — it was a great honour for me to be undertaking this project during Her Majesty's Diamond Jubilee year. The staff at the Royal Archives, especially Ms. Julie Crocker, was very helpful, despite undoubtedly being exceedingly busy during the celebrations of 2012.

On this side of the Atlantic I am grateful for the staff at Library and Archives Canada, Nova Scotia Archives, University of New Brunswick (Loyalist Collection), Hamilton Public Library, Special Collections and Archives at Brock University's James A. Gibson Library, and McMaster University (Mills Library).

One of my favourite periods of this project was spending two days sequestered in the Nova Scotia Archives (made possible by the hospitality and friendship of Christopher McCreery), pouring over the Jean Donald Gow Fonds, including her notes and unfinished manuscripts. I cannot underestimate how helpful Gow's research has been, and her voice echoes throughout my pages. I also owe a great debt to Dr. Mollie Gillen for her

Library and Archives Canada, Acc. No. R9266-190 Peter Winkworth Collection of Canadiana

What is believed to be Prince Edward's watercolour of a group of Mi'kmaq in Nova Scotia. This painting was included in a letter written by the Prince between 1796 and 1800 (neither the intended recipient nor the date are known).

thoroughly researched *A Prince and His Lady* (1970). Gillen's academic professionalism as she outlined the loving relationship between the Duke of Kent and Madame de St. Laurent provided me with a benchmark to emulate.

I am very proud that, like *Canada's Constitutional Monarchy* (Dundurn Press, 2010), this book features the art of Canadian icon Charles Pachter O.C. The cover image of the Duke of Kent comes from a painting commemorating Edward's 1792 meeting with Lieutenant Governor John Graves Simcoe in Newark during the first royal tour of Upper Canada. Painted in 2012, a print of this important work currently hangs in the vice-regal suite of the lieutenant governor of Ontario. I am indebted to Charles for allowing me the privilege of again using his art.

It is important to me to provide information that is accurate, and I am indebted to the following individuals and organizations for helping me present Prince Edward's story as truthfully and honestly as possible: Dr. Carolyn Harris, Reverend J. Lee Potter, Professor Thomas H.B. Symons, the Senate of Canada, Office of the Lieutenant Governor of Nova Scotia, The Historical Society of Ottawa and Heritage Ottawa (specifically David Jeanes).

As always, I am thankful to the guidance of Barry Penhale, publisher emeritus, and my indispensible editor Jane Gibson. Thanks to a constant stream of emails bridging Carlisle and Flesherton, the three of us spent our New Years together putting the final touches on this project.

Ever since meeting Kirk Howard, Dundurn president and publisher, at the very first Conference on the Canadian Crown in 2010, I have felt supported by both him and his exceptional team at Dundurn Press. I am very proud of my relationship with Dundurn, and appreciate the continued faith they have shown in me and my work.

My family was instrumental in getting this project completed on time. My amazing wife, Christine Vanderwal, and my daughters, Sophie and Elyse, were a constant source of encouragement and love. I must also mention my mother and father-in-law, Greta and Roy Vanderwal, who are two of the most selfless and loving people I have ever met. This past year has been full — loss of a beloved family cottage, purchase of a new home, growth of our extended family, and what could have been a life-changing car accident — and throughout all of it I have been so thankful of everyone's support in giving me the time I needed to disappear to Mills Library or head out to Nova Scotia for a few days.

Background

Political Divisions of British North America During the Duke of Kent's Time on the Continent, 1791–1800

British North America refers to the northern colonies that remained loyal to the Crown after the British accepted the independence of the United States of America in 1783. It is incorrect to refer to the entire region as "Canada," as not everyone living there identified with that name. Unofficially, Canada meant the lands encompassed by the Province of Quebec after the British Conquest of 1760. The Atlantic setters in Nova Scotia, Cape Breton Island, New Brunswick, Island of St. John (later rechristened Prince Edward Island), and Newfoundland did not see themselves as Canadian and would have identified with their local colony or province.

After the Constitution Act of 1791, which is discussed in this book, the old Province of Quebec was divided into Upper and Lower Canada — two separate provinces, sometimes collectively called "the Canadas." Even though after 1791 "Canada" was now being used in an official context, the term "Canadian"

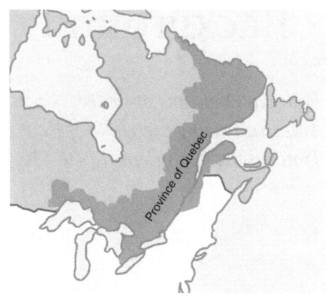

British North America before *(above)* and after *(below)* the Constitution Act of 1791.

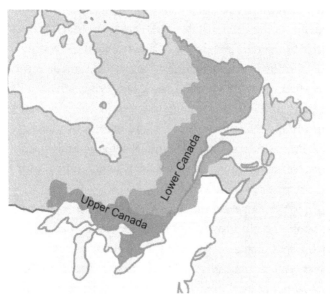

still meant a French settler in the eyes of most of the inhabitants (the Duke of Kent would begin to change this view). The British settlers, mainly Loyalists, would have referred to themselves as English, Scottish, Irish, or American, and the latter according to their former colonies of New York, Georgia, Maine, and so on.

This book discusses two very distinct regions — Canada (meaning Upper and Lower Canada) and the Atlantic colonies (mainly Nova Scotia). A unified "Canadian identity" would not develop until after Confederation. It is to be noted that the original purpose of the Charlottetown Conference in 1864 was to create a Maritime Union that did not include Upper or Lower Canada.

Introduction

Prince Edward, Duke of Kent

The story of Prince Edward Augustus, Duke of Kent (1767–1820), is also a story of early Canada. The Duke of Kent was not only a keen observer, but was also an active participant in the very genesis of the country. Canada's maps are dotted with the name of the Duke (Prince Edward Island being the most obvious example) — making him one of the most honoured among our forgotten historical figures.

Recently, I was given a tour of the historic Government House of Nova Scotia by its executive director (and private secretary to the lieutenant governor), Dr. Christopher McCreery. As he guided me through the storied — some official, some not so — rooms of that household I was reminded of an anecdote from Yann Martel's *Beatrice and Virgil*:

> Fiction and non-fiction are not so easily divided. Fiction may not be real, but it's true; it goes

beyond the garland of facts to get to emotional and psychological truths. As for non-fiction, for history, it may be real, but its truth is slippery, hard to access, with no fixed meaning bolted to it. If history doesn't become story, it dies to everyone except the historian.[1]

Office of the Lieutenant Governor of Nova Scotia.

The 1814 portrait of Prince Edward Augustus, Duke of Kent, by artist Sir William Beechey (1753–1839), hangs in the salon of Nova Scotia's Government House.

History begins somewhere between fiction and non-fiction, and this is true when speaking of the Canadian Crown. Our monarchy's story goes far beyond the official accounts and dates that pepper our history textbooks. Rather, it encompasses characters and anecdotes that instil a tour, like the one I was on in Halifax, with liveliness and meaning.

Often, historical figures are viewed as existing in isolation — in a sort of vacuum that keeps them from interacting with others. That John Graves Simcoe's father was a shipmate of James Cook, both serving with James Wolfe during the Seven Years' War (1756–63) surprises many. Lord Dorchester, governor general of the Canadas, distrusted the ambitions of Simcoe — a feeling he shared with Loyalist Sir John Johnson and American President George Washington. Mohawk Captain Joseph Brant not only met King George III on multiple occasions, he went on to befriend the Prince of Wales.

It is often forgotten that historical figures fought, loved, hated, and harboured jealousies among themselves, feelings that often crossed international boundaries. People also exaggerate, forget, and even outright lie in order to protect their legacies and versions of events. Historical narratives placed before us are simply the accepted interpretations and perspectives of the historians of the day.

On the second floor of Nova Scotia's Government House, neatly tucked into a corner of the peach-coloured salon, is a portrait of His Royal Highness, Prince Edward Augustus, Duke of Kent. To many on the tour this portrait may seem misplaced — the Duke died in 1820 as a seemingly obscure royal, the fifth child of King George III. However, this painting on the wall of Canada's oldest vice-regal residence acts as a signpost in our history, and very much has a place in the Nova Scotian and Canadian historical narratives.

Reading over the previous tomes detailing the life of Prince Edward Augustus (Jean Donald Gow's unfinished manuscript "HRH Prince Edward, Duke of Kent: Father to Victoria," Mollie Gillen's *The Prince and His Lady*, Roger Fulford's *Royal Dukes*, McKenzie Porter's *Overture to Victoria*, and William Naftel's *Prince Edward's Legacy*), I was struck by a great truth in history: once dead we are no longer in control of our identity. Past individuals who influenced their world also hoped to shape how they would be presented in the historical record, but no matter what their efforts may have been, once they left this world their stories became the property of others. Like scavengers on the site of a great shipwreck, historians pick at the debris left floating on the surface. Oftentimes they arrive with a story already in their minds, and limit their search for those artifacts that fit their version. If an artifact or anecdote is found that contradicts a particular narrative it will often be tossed back into the sea.

The Crown is an institution that is able to echo the society in which it exists. Such reflection is accomplished not only through the personality of the monarch, but also its representatives, officials, and the many different people who come in contact with the institution on a day-to-day basis. In a constitutional monarchy, such as the one developing during the eighteenth century in Canada, it is not the Crown that shapes society. Rather, it is the society that shapes and continually redefines the Crown. When considered from this perspective, the Duke of Kent becomes an excellent study. In looking at him we are forced to expand our gaze to those who were part of the extended community that surrounded Edward.

Over the past two hundred years, Prince Edward, Duke of Kent, has been cast as sadistic, romantic, naïve, oversexed, prudish, moronic, brilliant, adulterous, faithfully monogamous, and both a simpleton and military genius. Frequently, the biographies of the Duke of Kent have reflected the prevailing attitudes toward royalty at the times they were written. I must include myself in this list of authors who have not given the Duke of Kent, or his companion of twenty-seven years, Julie de St. Laurent, the attention they deserve. In my 2011 publication, *Canada's Constitutional Monarchy*, I incorrectly identified Madame de St. Laurent as Canadian rather than French, falling prey to the many popular histories that wrongly characterized her. In part, this book exists to atone for my earlier mistake.

The Duke of Kent is as much a figure of Canadian history as his contemporaries Elizabeth and John Graves Simcoe, Sir John and Francis Wentworth, Thomas Carleton, and Joseph Brant, and it is time that he be treated as such. The purpose of this book is to reclaim the Duke of Kent and return him to his rightful place in the Canadian historical narrative. It is appropriate that Edward would also end up fathering Queen Victoria — the Mother of Canada's "Great" (her word) Confederation.

The Duke of Kent spent nearly a decade in British North America, touring as much of it as he could. Officially here on a military posting, Edward also participated in the political and social worlds of the region and was a great promoter of the arts, particularly theatre and music. He was a great friend to French Canadians, cultivating relationships in Quebec that would endure for the remainder of his life. By touring Upper Canada eight months after its creation, he helped crystallize John Graves Simcoe's vision for a British nation at the heart of North America.

By 1799, the Duke of Kent was the commander-in-chief of all British North American forces — an office now combined with the role of governor general of Canada (an appointment that Edward once held aspirations for) — and settled in Nova Scotia. The Duke fortified key positions in the Maritimes in the lead up to the War of 1812, permanently marking the cityscapes of Halifax and Charlottetown. Charles-Michel de Salaberry, French-Canadian hero of the 1813 Battle of Châteauguay, was a close friend to the Duke, who, in turn, lobbied to ensure the lieutenant-colonel received the recognition he deserved.

Many historians credit the Duke of Kent as being the first to apply the term "Canadian" to both English and French inhabitants of the land — a key step in the formation of a collective identity for the British North American colonies. After permanently leaving Halifax after an accidental fall in 1800, Edward continued to correspond with Canadians, including letters to Jonathan Sewell (chief justice and speaker of the Lower Canadian Legislature) over his proposed union of British North America, fully fifty years before Confederation!

This book is titled *Prince Edward, Duke of Kent: Father of the Canadian Crown* for two reasons. The first is obvious: he went on to father, in the last year of his life, the sovereign under whom Canada confederated in 1867. The other reason is that the Duke's approach to monarchy established a template that still exists today. Edward's habit of touring the country as a personal representative of the King can be seen today in countless royal tours (his great-great-great-granddaughter Queen Elizabeth II has toured this country twenty-two times since ascending the throne in 1952). The Duke also held a strong belief that the Crown could act as a type of unifying superstructure for the various communities that inhabited British North America (during his time the major ones would have been the French, English, and First Nations), a belief still held today. The modern idea of the Canadian constitutional monarchy — the Crown as an umbrella under which

diverse provinces can be united and yet still interact as equals —
is emphasized in the speeches given by the Duke during his time
in the country, as well as members of the Royal family and their
Canadian representatives today. While the Canadian Crown did
not formally exist until the Statute of Westminster (1931), there
were various signposts that helped guide the institution to that
point. The Duke of Kent was one of the first such signposts.

If only Edward, shivering in the cold of his first Canadian
winter, could have foreseen that seventy years later the country
would be united under the crown of his daughter, Victoria —
Sir John A. Macdonald's "Queen of Canada."

Nathan Tidridge
Carlisle, Ontario

Forms of address used for Prince Edward in this book:

1767–1799: His Royal Highness The Prince Edward Augustus

1799–1820: His Royal Highness The Prince Edward Augustus, Duke of Kent and Strathearn, Earl of Dublin

Nova Scotia Archives. no.1987-453 no. 4380.

A 1796 portrait of His Royal Highness, Prince Edward, Duke of Kent that that was painted by Simon Weaver while Edward was stationed in Halifax. The original hangs in the Legislative Library of Province House, Halifax.

1

Fourth Son of the King, 1767

To say that King George III and Queen Charlotte performed their royal duties of producing enough heirs to secure the throne is an understatement: all told, thirteen of their children survived into adulthood.

With all the necessary witnesses and members of the Royal family nearby, Prince Edward Augustus arrived around noon on November 2, 1767. *The London Gazette* proudly proclaimed to the country: "Her Majesty is, God be praised, as well as can be expected; and the young Prince is in perfect Health."[1] Born at the residence of Queen Charlotte (on the site of what would become the modern edifice of Buckingham Palace), Edward is on record as being the largest baby she would ever have.

The infant prince was the newest member of the House of Hanover, the royal house of Great Britain since the death of the unhappy Queen Anne in 1714. Anne had no surviving offspring (despite seventeen pregnancies) to inherit the throne, and since the 1701 Act of Settlement barred Catholics from the British monarchy, the Crown passed to the granddaughter of King James I (he reigned 1603–25) Princess Sophia, Electress and Dowager Duchess of Hanover.[2] It was Sophia's son who became King George the first of the Hanoverians (and Edward's great-grandfather). Without the Act of Settlement, he would only have been 52nd in line to the throne.

Prince Edward's twenty-nine-year-old father was King George III. At that time he had only been on the throne for seven years of a reign that would last sixty years. Tall and slight, with the prominent eyes and large nose characteristic of the Hanoverians, George III may not have been remarkably handsome, but he was most certainly British. The first Hanoverian King to be born in England, George III was unique to his royal house in being the first monarch since Queen Anne to speak with an English accent — King George I didn't speak a word of English, and George II only did so with a thick German accent. Even though his ancestral lands ere in Hanover (the King was also styled "Elector of Hanover"), the fiercely British George III would never step foot in his German territories.

Courtesy of the Senate of Canada

Portrait of His Majesty, King George III, 1779, *artist Sir Joshua Reynolds (1723-1792). The painting hangs in the Senate of Canada. Legend has it that this portrait was donated by the King to thank the Canadian people for their loyalty.*

In another departure from the traditions of the Royal family of the time, George III remained faithful to his wife, Queen Charlotte, from the day he married her in 1761. Physically and mentally, the young King was in his prime at Edward's birth, unhindered by the madness — generally assumed to be caused by a hereditary blood disorder called porphyria[3] — that would afflict his final decades. Some of his doctors would attribute the King's eventual dementia to his fidelity to his wife!

George III had not been destined to become King until his father, Prince Frederick Louis, died of a burst abscess in his lung in 1751, making the twelve-year-old Prince George heir to the Crown of his grandfather, King George II. Young George was quickly proclaimed Prince of Wales that year. The final nine years of the reign of King George II were dominated by the world's first global conflict, the Seven Years' War (1754–63),[4] but it was his grandson who would ultimately oversee its conclusion.

The Seven Years' War began in North America as the French and Indian Wars, a series of conflicts along the frontier with British North America and involving such up-and-coming colonial officers as a young George Washington. Culminating on this continent with the epic Battle of the Plains of Abraham, the Canadian theatre of the war ended with the French governor general, the Marquis de Vaudreuil, surrendering to Lord Amherst (commander-in-chief of the British Forces in the continent) in Montreal on September 8, 1760.

One month after the fall of New France, King George II, suffering from chronic constipation, awoke early to drink his usual cup of hot chocolate. At 7:30 a.m. His Majesty was found slumped over his toilet after suffering a massive heart attack due to overexertion. It was a less than regal end to what had otherwise been a remarkable reign, and it was from that last throne that George II's grandson would inherit the Crown of Great Britain, becoming King George III on October 25, 1760. The new King's Canadian domain gained during the Seven Years' War was formalized with the 1763 Treaty of Paris, under which the vast North American empire of French King Louis XV was transferred to George III.

The vigour (not only in producing children) represented by the youthful King George III at Prince Edward's birth symbolized the rapidly expanding British Empire of the time — the new King had been embraced by his peoples (on both sides of the Atlantic). George III's growing family was the focus of much interest in the Empire (particularly in the Thirteen Colonies of North America) and each birth was eagerly celebrated.

Prince Edward Augustus was the fifth child, and fourth son, born to the King and Queen. When it was certain that the young Prince would survive, at least into early childhood, he was christened "Edward Augustus," after Prince Edward Augustus, Duke of York, the King's younger brother who had just died in Monaco. In fact, the Duke's body was lying in state at Westminster Abbey the day his namesake was born. In later years Prince Edward would confess to his chaplain, "My arrival was somewhat malapropos. Sometimes the thought has crossed me whether my inopportune appearance was not ominous of the life of gloom and struggle that awaited me."[5]

Despite being born under a cloud, Prince Edward seems to have enjoyed a close relationship with both his mother and father. The King and Queen were loving parents, spending much time reading and playing with their children. The stiff formality of public life melted away behind closed doors as the King took to the floor on hands and knees, galloping with his children around rooms littered with toys, books, pencils and colourful drawings. Reminiscing about the life of King George III during the year of his death, Ingrim Corbin, of the London Missionary Society, offers this warm anecdote:

> The King's affection for his children was peculiarly tender, and was strikingly exemplified in the anxious solicitude of his enquiries after them when indisposed. It is well-known, that he would personally go to the lower lodge [part of Queen Charlotte's residence], at the early hour of five in the morning, and, gently tapping at the door of their apartments, would enquire how they had passed the night.[6]

Even the King's oldest son, the Prince of Wales (and future George IV), whose relationship with his father would radically deteriorate in his adolescent years, was recorded playfully sneaking up to the King's door and yelling "Wilkes and No. 45 for ever!"[7] before running away to sounds of his father's laughter (John Wilkes, a noted English republican, journalist, and politician had been a constant thorn in the side of George III).

Sadly, this laughter would not echo too far into the lives of the King's sons. While the Princesses were always kept close to home (only three of the six were married off), a tradition existed in the House of Hanover of dysfunctional relationships between the men in the family — particularly between the reigning King and his oldest son. King George I hated the future George II,[8] who, in turn, would loath his heir, Prince Frederick. The same would be true for George III, especially in his relationship with his oldest son, Prince George Frederick.

As the boys grew up, the pious and monogamous lives lived by their parents would not be adopted by their sons, particularly the Prince of Wales and third son Prince William Henry (future William IV). Stories of the Princes visiting London's brothels and clubs enraged the devoutly Christian King, and the illegal marriage of the Prince of Wales to Roman Catholic Maria Fitzherbert (barred under the Royal Marriages Act of 1772 brought in by George III for just such an occasion) devastated his parents.

By the 1780s the Prince of Wales was surrounding himself politically with adversaries of his father — notably republican Charles James Fox,[9] the archrival of William Pitt the Younger (the King's prime minister). Within these circles the Prince of Wales was known for his mocking impressions of the King (especially when the King was suffering from one of his bouts of "madness") and hard drinking. Amassing a tremendous debt, thanks to his lifestyle, the Prince of Wales was ridiculed in the press for his overeating, excessive drinking, and womanizing. A read through the journals of Queen Victoria reveals numerous accounts of George's behaviour, both as Prince of Wales, and later as Prince Regent and King. Victoria recorded a conversation she had with Prime Minister Lord Melbourne (William Lamb) in which her mentor explained to the young Queen that he had never seen anybody eat or drink so much as George IV. The Queen quoted Melbourne, saying, "his spirits and love of fun [were] beyond everything."[10]

As each of his other sons grew into adulthood, George III feared that they would stray from him (and his example) and fall under the influence of the Prince of Wales. These fears forced the Royal family into a series of "camps," with some sons like Prince Augustus being favoured, and others, like Edward, being punished for straying too close to the lifestyles of their older brothers.

As well as being influenced by the toxic relationship developing between the King and the Prince of Wales, the young life of Prince Edward would also be dominated by the American Revolution. King George III is remembered as the man who lost the American colonies, and this must have hung heavily in the air as he played with his children on the floor of the Queen's Lodge. The American Declaration of Independence was issued when Edward was six years old, and the 1783 Treaty of Paris when he was sixteen. When news of King George's loss of America reached the ears of Russia's Catherine the Great (who had been asked by George III for soldiers to help defend Canada during the conflict — a request she refused), the Empress quipped: "Rather than have granted America her Independence as my brother monarch, King George, has done, I would have fired a pistol at my own head."[11]

Indeed, King George III was devastated by the loss of the Thirteen Colonies, even hoping for a great reconciliation and the reuniting of his kingdom. A 1783 draft of a speech to be given in Parliament, written by the King's own hand, survives. In it he announced his intention to abdicate and place himself into permanent exile in Hanover:

> A long experience and a serious attention to the strange Events that have successively arisen, has gradually prepared my mind to expect the time when I should be no longer of utility to this Empire; that hour has now come; I am therefore resolved to resign my Crown and all the Dominions appertaining to it to the Prince of

> Wales, my Eldest Son and Lawful Successor, and
> to retire to the care of my Electoral Dominions
> the Original Patrimony of my Ancestors.[12]

Ultimately, the King could not bring himself to leave Britain or relinquish his Crown, but it is clear that George III was tortured by his responsibility in losing America and this may have contributed to his short fuse in dealing with the antics of his sons.

In 1786, three years after the loss of America, King George III sent Prince Edward to the continent, placing him under the watchful eye of his older brother, Prince Frederick, Duke of York. Frederick, in turn, sent Edward to Lüneburg, assigning him to Lieutenant Colonel George Wangenheim, a trusted member of the Horse Guards. Given complete control over the Prince's finances, Wangenheim reported directly to the Duke of York, and was responsible for reading Edward's correspondences and managing his social engagements. Everywhere Edward travelled on the continent, Wangenheim was close behind.

Prince Edward seems to have been cursed with a weak constitution (in contrast with his father, who had never been sick, except for a brief illness in 1765), and a large portion of his letters home are preoccupied with reports of poor health. An undated note to his father complains: "The first lines which my hand is able to trace since my recovery from a violent rheumatism attended with fever, which nearly deprived me of total use of both my hands."[13] Edward would ultimately be settled in Geneva, Switzerland, where he could benefit from the clean air and pleasant climate.

Sadly, it was while Edward was in Europe that King George's bouts with "madness" developed, and the health of his sons became hot topics back in England. An unpublished manuscript by Nova Scotia historian Jean Donald Gow contends that many of George III's sons also showed signs of the same mental illness that afflicted their father — especially Princes Edward and Frederick.[14] Undoubtedly, these concerns would haunt the Royal family, particularly as the King's lapses into "madness" grew more frequent and violent during the close of the eighteenth century. Many of Edward's letters highlighting his many ailments to his father during his time in Europe went unanswered — particularly during the King's first bout of madness from 1787–89. It was during the autumn of 1788 that the King was found having a conversation with an oak tree, thinking that it was the King of Prussia.[15]

Isolated from his family in Geneva, Edward had grown to be a handsome six-foot-two-inch young man with penetrating blue eyes. As well as cutting a sleek profile in his military uniform, Edward, with the exception of the Prince of Wales, was considered the most intelligent of the brothers. A self-professed liberal, Prince Edward could carry conversations on a variety of topics if given the chance. Unlike his brothers, Edward also knew when to keep his mouth shut and had a capacity for quietness largely unknown to the Hanoverians. This silence, however, did not extend to the written word.

Quoting the Duke of Wellington, author Cecil Woodham Smith writes: "He united a pedantic love of detail with a love of interfering and setting right, and 'maintained an active and very extensive correspondence, which three or four private secretaries were scarcely able to master.… His name was never uttered without a sigh by the functionaries of every public office.'"[16]

Edward's correspondence was legendary — in 1806, he personally answered 3,850 letters without the aid of a secretary (for financial reasons he had dismissed them all by this time). In 1807, the number reached 4,500!

Away from his family, Prince Edward's day-to-day habits included rising at 5:00 a.m., eating sparingly, and avoiding at all costs gambling and excessive drinking. The Prince did, however, develop an interest in the opposite sex, and it was not long before Edward found himself in a series of affairs with women such as Marianne Dulaque (star of the Théâtré de la Place Neuve). A man of the Arts (he loved music and theatre), Edward also enjoyed the women he met on the stages across Geneva. Unable to suppress the Prince's youthful appetites, Wangenheim furiously wrote letters describing these affairs to the Duke of York, who passed them along to the King.

The final straw was Edward's 1789 affair with Adelaide Dubus, a local musician six years his senior. The affair grew (despite Wangenheim's efforts to have Dubus removed by Swiss authorities), and on December 15th the young musician died while giving birth to Edward's daughter, Adelaide Victoire Auguste. It fell to Edward's handlers, Wangenheim in particular, to clean up the mess. The Prince's daughter was placed into the care of Adelaide's sister, Victoire, who lived with her father Denis Dubus (both of whom were also musicians) and an annual subsidy was set up (50 guineas) with only a few conditions:

1. The child was to be given back to Edward if he requested it.
2. The child was to be brought up in the Protestant Faith.
3. The child was forbidden to become an actress.

Although Victoire Dubus appears in Genevan record books until 1832, Edward's first daughter died the following year on her way to Gibraltar. The child's aunt, in a vain attempt to fill the void in Edward's heart, brought the infant with her on the harsh Atlantic journey from Marseilles. While the Prince would continue to pay a pension to Victoire Dubus the rest of her life, she was never able to take the place of the mother of Edward's lost daughter.[17]

Edward had sustained his lifestyle in Geneva (including the cost of parties, mistresses, and the friends who tagged along) by incurring tremendous debts. (Some historians contend that Lieutenant Colonel Wangenheim incurred the debt on the Prince's behalf, while others assert that Edward made unrestrained financial commitments in protest of the close controls imposed by his handler.) Edward had discovered that no one minded lending money to a prince, but he failed to realize that ultimately people did expect to be repaid. Hearing reports of his son's behaviour in Geneva, George III must have been beside himself. With his mental health miraculously restored for the time being, the King was able to give his full attention to Edward's situation on the continent.

With creditors knocking at his door, and now the death of his mistress (while giving birth to his daughter), Edward panicked, and, going against Wangenheim's counsel, returned to England unannounced. Mollie Gillen writes that the Duke of York's agent tried in vain to dissuade the Prince from returning to his parents, but once he realized that Edward was determined to go home, Wangenheim wrote to King George III suggesting that "the Prince, feeling neglected by his father's failure to write for nearly two years, and seeking parental kindness rather than strict justice, hoped to explain his severe embarrassments in person."[18] The King would be in no mood to demonstrate such kindness.

When the disgraced and bankrupt Prince Edward arrived in London on January 13, 1790, the city was aghast. Edward had crossed Europe by coach using the last money he had, and now found himself in a small hotel, waiting for news of his request for an audience with his father. King George III was furious, and his son would not have to wait long for an answer.

Likely to his detriment, Edward had been immediately greeted in London by his brothers, the Prince of Wales and Prince William Henry, Duke of Clarence. They, along with the prime minister (William Pitt the Younger), lobbied the King to pity his son and grant him an audience. Finally relenting, the King permitted Edward a fifteen-minute interview on January 28th to explain his massive debts, illegitimate daughter, and dead lover.

No records of Edward's meeting with his father exist. No doubt the King looked at his son and saw the likelihood of Edward ending up like his older brothers — unless something drastic was done. It probably didn't matter what excuse Edward offered his father, since the King had already decided the fate of the Prince ten days before their tense meeting: by the 1st of February Edward would be on a ship bound for Gibraltar. King George could not be rid of his son fast enough, writing to his prime minister before meeting with the Prince, "With regard to the frigate for conveying Edward to Gibraltar I cannot think it so material whether he embarks preferably at Portsmouth or Plymouth as that he should as soon as possible quit London."[19]

Authors such as Roger Fulford (*Royal Dukes*, 1933) argue that the Prince's swift removal from England was the result of the King's hatred of his son. However, others such as Mollie Gillen suggest Edward was sent to "the Rock" by his father for his own protection — primarily from the influence of his older brothers. Aside from the Prince of Wales, King George's third son, Prince William Henry, was a prime example of someone Edward needed to avoid.

Although he would stay in British North America the longest of any member of the Royal family, Prince Edward was not the first royal to set foot on its shores; that distinction goes to his older brother, Prince William Henry. William's visits to British North America in 1786 and 1787 provide excellent snapshots of the behaviour that King George III deplored so much.

Courtesy of the Senate of Canada

Prince Edward's older brother William in later life after he had been crowned King William IV, engraving by Frederick Christian Lewis (1779–1856), from a drawing by Sir Thomas Lawrence (1769–1830).

Born on August 2, 1765, Prince William Henry is not remembered for his intellectual prowess. Nicknamed "Coconut Head" (some accounts describe him as "Pineapple Head") due to his enormous, conical forehead, William was a navy man through and through. Having joined the Royal Navy as a midshipman when he was thirteen years old, the young Prince found himself in New York City (and the focus of a kidnapping plot approved by George Washington) during the American Revolutionary War. By 1785 Prince William was given command of *HMS Pegasus*, becoming very close with Horatio Nelson during their time together in the Caribbean. It was in 1786 that *Pegasus* visited the Maritimes, carrying its famous royal commander to Newfoundland, Nova Scotia and Canada (Province of Quebec).[20] It was off the coast of Placentia, Newfoundland, that William turned twenty-one, and a lively account of the event is recorded in the journal of Sir Thomas Byam Martin:[21]

His Royal Highness lunched with the officers in the gun-room [now the ward-room], and the interchange of condescension on the one part and of love and loyalty on the other was so often plighted in a bumper[22] that by one o'clock scarcely one of the company could give distinct utterance to a word. By some means, I know not how (it was no easy matter), his Royal Highness contrived to crawl up to the main-deck, no doubt with the adventurous hope of being able to reach his cabin; but in an instant he was recognised by the seamen, all nearly as drunk as himself, who with unfeigned, irresistible loyalty, mounted him on their shoulders and ran with him violently from one end of the deck to the other. This was a most dangerous proceeding, for I am sure I may say that his head passed within an inch of the skids (beams) several times, and one blow at the rate they were going would inevitably have killed him ... I was too young to be admitted to the honour of the tipsy party, and, with three other dignitaries of my own standing, was instructed to take charge of the ship during the approaching interregnum, of which we were not a little proud.[23]

William's visits to Canada are filled with stories of debauchery and nights of binge drinking. Reading through the diary of Lieutenant William Dyott (stationed in Nova Scotia), the 1787 visit of William Henry starts with a note that the Prince disliked drinking very much, but ends with accounts of the royal party drinking sixty-three bottles of wine (shared among twenty people) in one night. Realizing his original mischaracterization of the Prince, Dyott's diary is peppered with accounts of William and others getting "very drunk," "completely drunk," "wondrous[ly] drunk," and "outrageously drunk."[24]

Prince William's visit to Halifax was also celebrated by the young women of the colony, including Frances Wentworth (wife of John Wentworth,[25] surveyor general of the King's Woods). Meeting William Dyott while on a walk through Halifax, the Prince took hold of the lieutenant's arm and resolved to visit all the young ladies in town. In his entry the following day, Dyott commented that the Prince would enter any house where he saw a pretty girl.[26] Dyott's entries concerning Frances Wentworth are even more interesting.

Upon Prince William's arrival to Halifax, John Wentworth left the town to take up his duties as surveyor-general. This allowed the Prince to visit the Wentworth residence whenever he liked, eventually eating and dressing there. Of Frances Wentworth, Dyott wrote: "Mrs. Wentworth is, I believe, a lady fonder of our sex than her own, and his [*sic*] Royal Highness used to be there frequently."[27] Later on in his diary, the lieutenant expanded his initial thoughts:

> Mrs. Wentworth is a most charming woman, but unhappily for her husband, rather more partial to our sex than her own. But he, poor man, cannot see her foibles, and they live very happy. I believe there was a mutual passion which subsisted between his [*sic*] Royal Highness and her. She is an American, but lived a good deal in England and with people of the first fashion.... I never laughed so much in my life; he was in vast spirits and pleasanter than anything I ever saw.... He dressed at Mrs. Wentworth's and went in her carriage, but not with her, as the ladies of Halifax are a little scrupulous of their virtue and think it in danger if they were to visit Mrs. Wentworth. For my part I think her the best-bred woman in the province.[28]

Much has been written about the open marriage enjoyed by the Wentworths, as well as Frances's — in the words of Nova Scotia historian Thomas Raddall — experience in the arts of the drawing room and bedchamber,[29] but Frances's relationship with Prince William assured the couple a degree of upward mobility. In fact, Frances Wentworth often travelled back to England, re-establishing old acquaintances and insuring preferential placement for both her and John Wentworth.

When Lieutenant Governor Jonathan Parr died of an apoplectic fit in 1791, the Wentworths were in England — Frances actively reacquainting herself with Prince William (now Duke of Clarence) — and John Wentworth was duly appointed the new representative of the King in Nova Scotia. Frances even had the honour of kissing the hand of George III.

Now back in England, Prince William was laying low for the time being, curbing some of his poor behaviour (which may have included his language, which was famous for its colourfulness) in an effort to draw favour from his father. It didn't matter — the King wanted William and his brother, the Prince of Wales, as far away as possible from Prince Edward.

Blindsided, Edward must have stood in shocked silence as he watched the coastline of England fade away. After a whirlwind attempt to come home, Edward would not see his family for another eight years.

2

Exiled to the Rock, 1791

The British territory of Gibraltar is located at the strategic Atlantic mouth of the Mediterranean Sea. Whoever controls this piece of real estate jutting out of Spain (at its narrowest, the peninsula measures only half a mile in width, at its greatest, three-quarters of a mile), dominated by its great 1,350-foot "Rock," is master of all that flows in and out of the western entrance to the southern waterway of Europe. Since the Treaty of Utrecht in 1714, Gibraltar has been a territory of the British and the site of one of its key military bases. A 1782 volume describes the settlement as "situated at the foot of the mountain, and afforded a handsome appearance, the houses having been in general well-built of the rock stone, and the streets neatly paved."[1] According to British Prime Minister William Pitt the Younger, Gibraltar was the most inestimable jewel of the British Crown during the eighteenth century.[2]

On February 24, 1790, Prince Edward Augustus arrived in Gibraltar to assume command of the Queen's Royal Regiment.

The colony was awash in alcohol, and the young Prince was charged with bringing its rowdy occupants back in line — a tall order in a territory with little else to do but drink.

The Queen's Royal Regiment was originally named the Tangiers Regiment when it was raised in 1661 to garrison Tangiers, part of the dowry of the Portuguese Princess Catherine of Braganza, who married England's King Charles II the following year. The regiment was renamed "The Queen's Regiment," after Queen Catherine, when it was returned to England in 1684. Prior to being posted to Gibraltar, the regiment was active in England, Ireland, and/or the European continent. Sent to North America in 1711, during the War of the Spanish Succession (1701–1714), the regiment eventually found its way back to England, until it was posted to Gibraltar from 1730–1749. The regiment was again returned to the Rock in 1783.[3]

With the Prince also came the Royal Fusiliers (the 7th Regiment of Foot). Edward had been appointed the regiment's colonel in 1789 when it was quartered at Glasgow and the Isle of Man, and it now followed him to King George's most strategic outpost in the Mediterranean.

The Royal Fusiliers had a rich history before coming under the command of Prince Edward. Connected with the Tower of London, the regiment started as a Tower Guard raised by James II in 1685. The company was styled by King James as "Our Royal Regiment of Fuzileers [*sic*]" because they were initially armed with flintlock — or "fuzil" — muskets. In 1751, the regiment was renamed "The 7th Regiment of Foot (Royal Fusiliers),"[4] bringing it into line with the new policy of numbering English regiments to show their seniority, or reflecting their formation date or the date that the regiment (if formed outside of England) was made a part of the English Establishment.[5]

The Royal Fusiliers had unique traditions that are worth noting. Originally, the officers for this regiment were taken from other established units, earning the Fusiliers the nickname "Elegant Extracts." This policy of recruiting from other regiments would be adopted by Prince Edward, to the chagrin of many, including John Graves Simcoe. As with other London-based regiments, the Royal Fusiliers had the privilege of marching through the city with their drums beating, colours flying, and bayonets fixed. Another honour would be granted by Edward's brother, King William IV, when he allowed the regiment the privilege of never having to drink the Loyal Toast in the officer's mess, because "the loyalty of the officers of the Royal Fusiliers was beyond question."[6]

The regiment already had an illustrious association with British North America, participating in many of the campaigns of the American Revolutionary War. Deployed to the continent early in the conflict, in 1773, the Royal Fusiliers helped repel (even though all but one company was taken prisoner and sent to Philadelphia) the attempted rebel invasions of the Province of Quebec in 1775 and 1776. In fact, it had been the remnants of the Royal Fusiliers (along with Royal Highland Emigrants, marines, sailors, and Canadien militia and volunteers) that had ultimately prevented the American army from marching on Quebec. The Royal Fusiliers also saw service throughout the Great Lakes and surrounding area, including forts St. John, Chambly (where the regiment was defeated, their colours captured and sent to the Continental Congress — considered the first war trophy of its kind of the American Revolution[7]), Clinton, and Montgomery. They also saw action during the Philadelphia Campaign, Monmouth Court House, Charleston and Cowpens, Savannah, and New York City, where the regiment stayed until the British departed in 1783.[8]

It was as commander of both the Royal Fusiliers and the Queen's Royal Regiment that the image of Prince Edward as a severe disciplinarian appears in many popular accounts of his military career. In fact, if not carefully examined, it would seem that the Prince's obsession with (and suggested enjoyment of) flogging his soldiers is one of the few agreements that historians have concerning Edward's life. Roger Fulford writes in *Royal Dukes* that Prince Edward "rose from bed early to inspect, drill and to order floggings," and that men chaffed under his tyranny.[9] Even though Fulford's assertions have been successfully challenged by other historians — notably Mollie Gillen — they still crop up from time to time. The reality is that the British Army of the late eighteenth century was a brutal institution that had, at its heart, a strict code of discipline. Section XIV of the 1791 manual *The Elements of Military Arrangement, and of Discipline of War; Adapted to the Practice of the British Infantry*, explained the rationalization for severe punishment in the military:

> Punishments being intended to deter by the terror of example, and not so much to vindicate, as to prevent, the commission of crimes, it follows, that they should be most pointed on those, for which the most frequent opportunities and the most prevailing temptations offer ..."[10]

As far as what punishments were at the disposal of Prince Edward, the manual was quite clear: "The principal punishments now inflicted on private soldiers by military law, are flogging on the back or shoulders with a cat of nine tails; imprisonment in the guard-house, or [the] black-hole ..."[11] Although the practice would be abolished with the Army Act of 1881, flogging was considered the bedrock of the British Army. In fact, during the period of Prince Edward's service, official statistics reveal that punishments of 1,500 lashes (although by 1807 all punishments could not exceed 1,000 lashes) were not uncommon in the army.[12]

As well as the cat-o'-nine-tails, more imaginative options were available for a commander to inflict on his regiment. However, these disciplinary tactics were falling into disuse by the eighteenth century and would not continue into the nineteenth. These alternative disciplines included:

- Hanging an individual by their thumbs so that only their toes could touch the ground.
- Picketing: forcing a man to stand with one leg on a wooden peg.
- Riding the wooden horse: a man sits suspended with two planks forming a sharp edge running between his legs with heavy weights tied to each foot.
- Boring a hole through a soldier's tongue with a red-hot poker.
- The strappado: tying a man's hands behind his back, and raising him up using a rope tied to his wrists — the rope would be immediately slackened, allowing the man to free-fall to the ground, before being quickly tightened, causing his shoulders to be dislocated.
- Running the gantlet: a soldier is forced to run between two rows of their fellow soldiers armed with various weapons including cudgels and/or clubs.
- Branding of the forehead and arms.[13]

Executions were also very common, with the preferred methods being a firing squad or hanging from a long branch of a tree, while some European counterparts of the British Army still practised beheading (for executions that were meant to be "honourable"). The British infantry stationed in Holland practised "clubbing" (suspending a soldier's corpse by their feet after their execution), but one of the most unique forms of execution was particular to the British forces in India:

> There is a species of execution practiced by our company's troops in India, which seems more suitable to a soldier, and a more honourable punishment that any ... blowing them from the mouth of a cannon: this while it appears to be easy and unexcruciating [*sic*], must certainly be acknowledged a very military execution.[14]

A soldier condemned to death by firing squad would be dressed in white and marched (while his regimental band played the death march) to his execution site behind four men carrying his coffin. Once there, the coffin was placed in a freshly dug grave. Kneeling on his coffin, the condemned man would have the option, if he wished, of having a nightcap placed over his eyes before being shot at close range by his brother soldiers. All of this would be witnessed by the regiment, whose involvement also included a slow march past the corpse post-execution.

Prince Edward was a product of his time, and while he may have been obsessed with military protocol, accusations that he was sadistic and took pleasure in flogging his men are misplaced. At the time of his arrival in Gibraltar, the outpost was drowning in alcohol and lacked any sort of discipline and order. Edward's attempts to try and restore order to the outpost, particularly by closing many of the pubs and wine houses, was immediately met with hostility. As an 1875 history of the Royal Fusiliers explained, in Gibraltar "great slackness existed, and when the young [Prince Edward] attempted to exact proper and honourable performance of his duty from each of his subordinates, his measures were received with great and ill-conceived disgust."[15]

That the Prince would only last six months in Gibraltar had more to do with his health concerns than the British government trying to get rid of an uncontrollable disciplinarian. The Rock's location, strategic as it is, also ensures it a climate that becomes oppressively hot. The thick heat, dampened by the Mediterranean, hangs heavily over the colony during the summer months. Such weather agitated Edward's weak constitution and provoked a flood of letters back to his father, begging for reassignment: "[M]y health has so very materially suffered during the immoderate heat of this last summer that the Surgeon General of our Garrison … has given it as his positive opinion that by my remaining here another summer my health would be exposed not only to the most prejudicial but perhaps the most fatal attacks."[16]

For nearly two centuries it has been maintained by many authors and historians that Prince Edward was exiled to Canada (specifically Quebec City) because of the poor treatment of his regiment in Gibraltar. The image of the Prince being flung to the furthest corner of the British Empire, an alien French culture where English royalty were seen as "conquerors," supports a popular narrative that isolates the Crown from Canadian history. The Crown is often portrayed in Canadian history books as distant and aloof — present only in fleeting royal tours (routinely called simply "visits") and images of nineteenth and early-twentieth-century Anglo-Canada. The idea that a prominent member of the Royal family would have lived in Canada — in Quebec no less — at a crucial point in its formative history, and participating directly in that formation, is a notion that most Canadians are surprised to learn. More importantly, it needs to be understood that Prince Edward was not sent to Canada against his will, but actually requested his posting to Quebec.

Plagued by the heat of Gibraltar, Edward appealed to his father for relief — even alluding to a connection between his bouts of ill-health and the King's own struggle with mental illness. While Prince Edward's hope was always to return to his family in England, he knew that was not possible for the foreseeable future, and, instead of campaigning for a new assignment, he threatened to leave his regiment if an alternate posting was not offered (this would not be the last time he would threaten this tactic). Writing to his father on December 13, 1790, Edward pleaded:

> Nothing would give me more pain than my being at present obliged to quit the Regiment I have now the honor of commanding. I therefore presume to hope that your Majesty, actuated in partly by consideration of the unfortunate state of my health in this climate, as well as the infinite advantage of which my removal to a colder one will be to me, will not refuse my request when I petition that if it does not interfere with your commands for other Regiments in your service, you will allow me to be sent in the Spring with mine **to any part of North America which you may chuse to appoint; allowing me, if it means with your approbation, to prefer Canada.**[17] [bolding by author]

A further letter was sent by the Prince to his father on January 24, 1791, reminding the King of the request to be posted with the Royal Fusiliers to Canada. On February 14, the Gibraltar Garrison Orders announced that Edward and his regiment were to be moved to Quebec.

On May 11, 1791, a grand ball was held in honour of the departing Prince at Gibraltar's Hotel de l'Europe. The lavish affair was attended by officers of the Royal Navy and the British Army, as well as guests from the Dutch and Portuguese navies. A specially constructed room for 240 guests (another room nearby held more) was built on the ruins of an old barracks next to the hotel. Adorned with a pink canopy of silk with silver ornaments, the room was dominated by a figure of Fame holding the English ensign. The Prince's seat was crowned with an illuminated representation of a rising sun. The sides of the canopy, near the Prince, were occupied by representations of Minerva and Fame. During those celebrations a boy in the Queen's Royal Regiment sang a composition lamenting Edward's departure from the Rock:

> So fades our joy round Calpe's[18] brow,
> For Royal Edward leaves us now!
> 'Twas he who taught us how to bear
> The soldier's toil, the leader's care;
> Yet cheered fatigue with festive hours
> And strewed war's rugged path with flowers.
>
> Ye breezes waft him safely o'er
> To brave the cold Canadian shore!
> To spread afar his rising fame
> And make his own a glorious name![19]

Prince Edward finally departed Gibraltar aboard HMS *Resistance* on May 27, 1791. Nova Scotia historian Mollie Gillen's book *The Prince and His Lady* lists, on the ship's muster roll, a name that would be forever linked with Edward's: Madame de St. Laurent. Named Alphonsine Julie Thérèse-Bernardine de Montgenêt, Baronne de Fortisson, Prince Edward's mistress has become known to history as Madame "Julie" de St. Laurent. A curious letter from Prince Edward dated June 5, 1790, survives in Arthur Aspinall's published correspondence of the Prince of Wales, gives the reason for Madame de St. Laurent's inclusion on the *Resistance*'s roster: "there is one essential requisite towards rendering the life of a young soldier happy, in a solitary place like this, I mean, a partner for his leisure hours, which seldom, *selon mon gout* ["according to my taste"], I am incapable to provide myself with here..."[20] What Aspinall edited out (and the Royal Archives were able to fill in) speaks to the desperation of Edward's loneliness and that his needs were not simply sexual: "You know, that is a point, I am not easily satisfied about; for I despise every sensual enjoyment, which one might procure when the object of it is a prostitute, in short I look for a companion, not for a whore."[21]

Canadians have been fascinated by the relationship between these two people ever since their arrival in Quebec. Interestingly, each biography published about Edward has its own particular interpretation of his relationship with Julie.

Published in 1962, McKenzie Porter's *Overture to Victoria* is perhaps the most colourful account of the pair. Porter's account of the Prince reads like a novel, complete with embellishments deemed necessary to keep the reader's interest. Madame de St. Laurent is presented as the childhood friend of Marie Josèphe Rose Tascher de la Pagerie (the future Josephine, wife of

Napoleon) and Porter maintains that records of Julie's relationship with Edward were suppressed in later years by an embarrassed Queen Victoria — an elaborate royal cover-up that was never supposed to see the light of day. The Julie of *Overture to Victoria* seems to mirror Wallis Simpson,[22] zeroing in on the young Prince Edward with the tacit approval of her husband, the Baron de Fortisson (they were both in need of royal patronage since being exiled and bankrupted by the French Revolution). The Baron parted from the couple (leaving Julie with their daughter, Melanie, who vanishes from the historical record in 1798) before their arrival in Quebec. The Baron de Fortisson was eventually decapitated by a cannonball while fighting against the French in the West Indies in 1797. In Porter's book, it is Prince Edward, of course, who makes the grisly discovery. The author emphatically asserts, "This extraordinary coincidence is vouched for by a direct descendant of Edward and Julie."[23] Porter's source was an unnamed gentleman, who had heard the story from his father, who himself had been told by his great-grandmother, Julie de St. Laurent.

Mackenzie Porter alleges that two sons were born to the couple: Robert Wood (born in Quebec City and subsequently raised by Edward's former personal servant of the same name) and Jean de Mestre (born en route to Halifax and raised by Julie's mother in Martinique). Both sons thrived, populating Canada and Australia (Jean de Mestre's final home) with their own quasi-royal descendants. After the death of Prince Edward, Julie eventually remarried and found herself back in Quebec with her new husband, a Russian-Italian prince named Prospero Colonna. Julie's second prince was eventually lost at sea, leaving the twice-widowed Madame to finish her days at her old holiday home at Montmorency Falls, periodically being visited by the descendants of her and Edward's sons, and dying at the ripe old age of 106.[24] All of this is romantic, fantastic, but utterly fictitious! For a much more factual account of the twenty-seven-year relationship between Edward and his Madame de St. Laurent, Mollie Gillen's meticulous tome is a must-read.

The Prince's beloved companion came into his life just before he requested his transfer from Gibraltar. Edward had dispatched his valet to Europe to locate a female companion who could relieve his loneliness on the Rock. While there certainly was a physical dimension to this mission, the Prince was more concerned with finding a companion than simply a lover.

Colonel Richard Symes, who, despite his pleas not to be, was appointed by King George III to keep an eye on Edward in Gibraltar. In his line of duty, he wrote countless letters back to England describing the Prince's idleness. However, a letter written on December 27, 1791, from Symes to Lord Grenville, British home secretary, makes it clear that the Prince had found something to occupy his time — but someone his handler did not approve of: "[A] Lady has just arrived whose company here at present would have been very well dispensed with. Had she arrived five months since, her coming might have had a good effect, and have prevented what has nearly produced a great deal of mischief, which to avert in part has cost me both infinite pains and extreme anxiety." All of this preceded a very interesting line: "The Prince at present talks of her going with him from hence, but before that can take place I hope he will grow tired of her, and move without the Embarras [*sic*] of such an Incumbrance [*sic*]."[25]

Edward, however, did not grow tired of Julie de St. Laurent, who was four years his senior, and she followed him across the Atlantic to the grey edifice of Quebec. Their relationship would span nearly three decades, and Julie would prove to be a stabilizing force in Edward's life. After meeting Edward's companion for the first time in 1794, Sir John Wentworth, then the lieutenant governor of Nova Scotia, wrote to his friend John King, the British undersecretary of state:

> Madame de St. Laurent (with a hundred names & titles) … is an elegant, well bred, pleasing sensible woman — far beyond most. During her residence here, her deportment has been judicious and most perfectly correct indeed. I find she has a great influence over him [Prince Edward] and that he is extremely attached to her. It is happy that she is so excellent a character. By her prudence and cleverness she has restored his deranged finances, and I believe, impressed his mind with the best sentiments.… I never yet saw a woman of such intrepid fortitude yet possessing the finest temper and refined manners.[26]

Julie, born around 1764 as Thérèse-Bernardine de Montgenêt, was raised in Besançon, France, near the Swiss border in Franche-Comté. The middle child of five born to Claudine Pussot and Jean Mongenêt, an engineer in France's department of highways, she had a quiet childhood, although her early adulthood would be dominated by the violence of the French Revolution.

By 1786, the twenty-two-year-old Thérèse-Bernardine de Montgenêt had become the mistress of French aristocrat Philippe Claude Auguste de Chouly, Marquis de Permangle. Bankrupted after having all of his assets seized during the Revolution, the Marquis and his mistress travelled around

Europe looking for work. However, by 1790 there was no more money left to support Thérèse-Bernardine, and the Marquis had to part ways with her in Malaga, Spain.[27] It was here that she met Prince Edward's valet, known to history only as M. Fontiny (or Fantiny). By November 23, 1790, the former mistress of the Marquis de Permangle was in Gibraltar, and, within six months, was on her way to Canada. From this point on, the French mistress is referred to as Madame de St. Laurent. Mollie Gillen writes that only the faintest clues reveal the name "Julie,"[28] the name given to her by Edward.

The source of her name as "St. Laurent" has been lost over time, but there are numerous possibilities in the eponyms of Canada. A romantic possibility could be found in the Île d'Orléans (called Minigo — the Enchantress — by the region's First Nations peoples), located in the St. Lawrence east of Quebec City. This island was referred to as Saint-Laurent (as well as La Grande Île and Sainte-Marie) during the seventeenth and eighteenth centuries.[29] Perhaps a more obvious suggestion could be that Edward named his mistress after the great river of Canada — the great seaway to the treasures of the continent.

Prince Edward must have sighed in relief as his ship pointed west and the great rock of Gibraltar bowed below the horizon. With Julie de St. Laurent at his side, Edward was heading even further away from his family and home. Ahead of him lay the remains of British North America, as well as a young, hot-blooded United States. Three days before Edward boarded the *Resistance*, American diplomat Charles F.W. Dumas (living in the Dutch Republic) sent an encoded message from The Hague to Thomas Jefferson (then America's first secretary of state) reporting: "Prince Edward has gone from Gibraltar to Quebec with his regiment to extend its fortifications. Why? To hold the Canadians in check?

Do they fear the Americans or the French? Neither will be aggressors."[30] Before even arriving, Edward's presence was grabbing people's attention in the New World.

3

Quebec, 1791

On August 11, 1791, seven weeks after leaving Gibraltar, HMS *Resistance* glided up the St. Lawrence on its way to the old capital of New France. Set atop a great precipice, the settlement of Quebec claimed a population of 2,255 Catholics and 790 Protestants.[1]

The morning after their arrival, the twenty-three-year-old Prince Edward Augustus stood on the deck of *Resistance* gazing up at the citadel atop the great escarpment. Dressed in his red tunic as commander of the Royal Fusiliers, the Prince would have been easy to spot from the shore as he looked out into the country that would become his home for the better part of the next decade. He immediately wrote to his father: "I have the honor of informing your [*sic*] Majesty that after a voyage of seven weeks, we anchored off Quebec on the 11th of August, late in the evening." His insecurities and lack of confidence are revealed as he continued:

I hope you will allow me, Sir, to express how grateful I shall feel if your [*sic*] Majesty will favor me with a line under your own hand that my conduct in Gibraltar has met with your approbation. To merit that is my highest ambition, and I trust, whatever unfortunate prejudice you may at the former period have felt against me [a reference to Edward's disastrous conduct in Geneva], the line of behavior I there pursued, and which I shall critically follow there, will remove it.[2]

It would seem that Edward had much in common with his new home, a country he would later commit to staying in for two years. Both the Prince and the land that would become Canada were seeking to establish an identity, and with it a confidence that would carry them into the future.

Edward, disgraced in Geneva and hopelessly in debt, had been banished indefinitely by his father and no longer had a place within the Royal family. For Canada, only thirty years had passed since the Battle of the Plains of Abraham and Articles of Capitulation had transformed the region into a British territory, and only a scant eight years since the Treaty of Paris confirmed the independence of the United States of America. Although British North America by name, the territory was largely populated by French Canadians whose mother country had been thrown into the flames of the French Revolution and would emerge as fiercely republican. The France in the minds of the *Canadienes* no longer existed — its royal fleur-de-lis ripped down as the country headed down a path that would ultimately lead to a bloody revolution and the Napoleonic Wars.

Following the American Revolution, the British colonies (Newfoundland, Nova Scotia, New Brunswick, the Province of Quebec, and St. John's Island) remaining in the New World were thinly populated and had little in common with one another. An aura of unease was particularly prevalent among Quebec's English-speaking settlers, who viewed their French co-inhabitants with a suspicious eye. In fact, many of the newer settlers in the Province of Quebec were American farmers lured to the region by cheap land. It is said that while these new settlers swore allegiance to King George III in order to secure this land, they did so with their fingers crossed behind their backs.

By the fact of simply being there, Prince Edward would become a symbol for many English-speaking settlers of the country — particularly the Loyalists and the new class of empire-builders, such as John Graves Simcoe, who were steadily trickling into the continent. Through Edward, there would be a tangible link not only to Great Britain, but to the King himself.

However, the initial precariousness of a member of the Royal family living in British North America cannot be over-stated. By its very nature the Crown acts as a symbol, but what it actually represents depends on the community in contact with it. Proximity changes the nature of a symbol — for Canadian society the King had always been a distant figure left to the interpretation of his representatives and subjects. But, by appearing on the Canadian shoreline in 1791, Prince Edward would create relationships with the Crown that would link many of the region's diverse communities — the First Nations, French, English, and other settlers — through personal contact, a template that is still used in Canada today in modern royal tours. Still, such a role is a political minefield, and, as Thomas Ashton Coffin, the American-born Loyalist secretary to Lord Dorchester, warned in a letter during the arrival of Edward to the country, "A Prince of the Blood cooped up in Quebec I imagine will be uncomfortable and make those around him so to[*sic*]."[3]

Edward, always aware of his station as the son of the King, would have enjoyed the opportunity not only to represent the Crown in Canada, but also to prove himself worthy of such a responsibility. As the *Resistance* dropped anchor in the St. Lawrence near Quebec City, the Prince prepared to immerse himself in a collection of people who would use him to create what they saw as the emerging identity of Canada. At the same time he would use his residence in North America to prove to his father that he, Edward, was a model military figure and member of the Royal family.

While travelling up the St. Lawrence the evening before, Edward would have noticed the river narrowing as it approached the settlement at Quebec. Founded by Samuel de Champlain[4] in 1608, the settlement had acquired its name from the Iroquoian word *kebec*, meaning "the narrowing of the waters." Essentially a peninsula ringed by an escarpment, Quebec is hemmed in by the St. Charles River to the north and the St. Lawrence to the south.

Archives Ontario, F 47-11-3-3.

Elizabeth Simcoe's sketch of the settlement at Quebec during her approach aboard the Triton *in 1791. Both the upper and lower sections of the settlement are clearly visible.*

The approach to the city may have reminded Prince Edward of Gibraltar, except that crowning the North American "Rock" were the great walls of the city of Quebec, which protected the Châteaux Saint-Louis and Haldimand, both residences of Lord Dorchester (Guy Carleton), governor-in-chief of the Province of Quebec.

In 1791, Quebec City was divided into two sections — the Upper and Lower Town. Elizabeth Simcoe, wife of John Graves Simcoe, arriving in the city on a cold and rainy day three months after the Prince, made the following entry about the settlement in her famous diary:

> Quebec is divided into Upper & Lower town. The latter is inhabited by Merchants for the Convenience of the Harbour & Quays. They have spacious Houses 3 stories high built of dark stone, but the streets are narrow & gloomy. In the suburbs of St. Roc are ruins of the Intendant's Palace[5] which is a very large building. The Upper Town is more airy & pleasant though the Houses in general are less … The Chateau, the Residence of the Governor,[6] contains some very good rooms built by Sir Frederick Haldimand.[7] The situation is very high & commands a most noble prospect down the River. The old Chateau[8] is in a ruinous state but is used for publik [*sic*] offices & convenient for the Gov. as being so near his own Residence that there is only a Court Yard between them.[9]

Even though the region had been known to Europeans for nearly three centuries, by 1791 it was still considered wild and largely unexplored. Dr. John Mervin Nooth,[10] the inspector general of hospitals in Quebec, corresponded regularly with Captain James Cook's famous botanist, Sir Joseph Banks, and frequently enclosed numerous specimens of local plants and even samples of First Nations' earthenware. He repeatedly commented to Banks about earthquakes felt in Quebec, believing they were caused by an undiscovered volcano thought to be still burning in the mountains to the northeast of the city. When voyagers returned from Quebec's hinterland, Nooth would wait to hear of evidence proving the volcano's existence.[11] His speculations regarding a volcano near Quebec City were also noted by Elizabeth Simcoe.[12]

There was little ceremony to greet the son of King George III when he landed on the shores of Quebec. Escorted up to Château Saint-Louis, overlooking the St. Lawrence, Prince Edward was formally greeted by Governor Lord Dorchester, Lieutenant Governor Sir Alured Clarke, and the rest of the colonial elite, including individuals such as seigneur Louis de Salaberry and lawyer Jonathan Sewell, with whom he would form lasting friendships.

Born in 1724 in Strabane, County Tyrone, Ireland, General Sir Guy Carleton, Lord Dorchester, was at the very centre of British North American society. A friend of then-Lieutenant James Wolfe,[13] Carleton had fought for the British during the War of the Austrian Succession (1740–48), becoming aide-de-camp to Prince George Augustus (Duke of Cumberland, son of George II). Thanks to the patronage of Wolfe, Carleton moved up the ranks after the war.

When the Seven Years' War began, James Wolfe (now a brigadier general) and Major-General Jeffery Amherst, commander-in-chief of British North American Forces from 1758 to 1763, wanted the Irishman to join them in the siege of the French Fortress of Louisburg on Cape Breton Island. However, thanks to some unfortunate comments Carleton had made about the quality of Hanoverian troops, which had found their way to the ear of King George II, the lieutenant-colonel's request to join his friends was denied.

Upon his return to England after his victory at Louisburg in 1758, Wolfe was given the title major-general and ordered to push on to Quebec City. Submitting his list of men required for the expedition to George II, Wolfe again tried to include his friend, Carleton. Finally, after a third request was submitted, the King relented and the Irishman was on his way to the Plains of Abraham.

It was while his men stormed the thick walls of Quebec that a French bullet pierced Major-General Wolfe's chest on September 14, 1759. At almost the same time Carleton was also wounded — struck in the head. The loss of Wolfe was devastating to his protégé, and Carleton returned to England in 1761 after the collapse of French forces in North America.

Carleton's military career, however, soared after his participation in the defeat of New France, and he now found favour with the newly crowned King George III. His participation in a brilliant 1762 campaign against the Spanish in Havana, Cuba, assured him of the esteem of King and country, and Carleton found himself back in Quebec as brigadier general and lieutenant governor in 1766. He would be elevated to governor in 1768 despite having no experience in civil government.

It was Governor Carleton who heavily influenced the framing of the 1774 Quebec Act, preserving French laws and the Roman Catholic faith in the province. He retired to England in 1778, but was asked to return to the North American continent to oversee the evacuation of Loyalists from New York in 1782 until the last British troops departed on November 25, 1783. (The city celebrated this event as Evacuation Day every

November 25 until the end of the First World War. In 2008, beacons were lit, mimicking bonfires, for the two hundredth anniversary of the British departure.) Ennobled as Lord Dorchester, a reward for a job well done, Guy Carleton was again returned to North America in 1786, this time as governor-in-chief of Britain's remaining northern colonies. While in his role as governor, Lord Dorchester created one of the only hereditary titles in North America when, on November 9, 1789, he proclaimed:

> Those Loyalists who have adhered to the unity
> of the Empire, and joined the Royal Standard
> before the Treaty of Separation in the year 1783,
> and all their children and their descendants by
> either sex, are to be distinguished by the follow-
> ing capitals, affixed to their names: U.E. alluding
> to their great principle the unity of the Empire.[14]

Shortly after his brief formal welcome to the province, Lord Dorchester presented Prince Edward to a delegation of forty First Nation leaders headed by Sir John Johnson, who, since 1782, had been the "superintendent general and inspector general of the Six Nations Indians and those in the Province of Quebec." Edward was also introduced to the well-known Captain Joseph Brant (Thayendanegea) of the Six Nations.

The son of Sir William Johnson (circa 1715–July 11, 1774), commander of the Iroquois and colonial militia forces in the Mohawk Valley during the Seven Years' War, Sir John Johnson became one of the most highly regarded Loyalists in Canada, a friend to both the First Nations (he had been appointed superintendent general of Indian Affairs in 1782 by Governor Haldimand)

and the English settlers. Johnson embodied the main conduit of information between the Crown and the region's First Nations, a relationship that included a friendship with Joseph Brant (Brant's sister Molly was Johnson's stepmother). By siding with the British during the American Revolution, Johnson had forfeited nearly 200,000 acres of land in New York (valued at nearly £184,000).[15] Ontario historian Brigadier General E.A. Cruickshank would later explain: "His possessions in the State of New York were as extensive and valuable as those of any colonial resident of his time … and no other person in America imperilled and lost more by his loyalty to the Crown."[16]

Although not documented, it is possible that Prince Edward knew that Johnson had been Lord Dorchester's choice as the first lieutenant governor of Upper Canada. As early as 1784 Governor Haldimand had written to Johnson assuring him that he would put his name forward to be "appointed Lieut. Gov. & Commandant of that District & Superintendant General of the Refugee Loyalists therein,"[17] but implored him to keep this promise secret. After his appointment to the governorship of the Canadas, Lord Dorchester upheld the pledge made by Haldimand, only to have it rejected by William Grenville, the British home secretary, on the grounds that Johnson was too close to the people and owned too much land to possess the balance needed for such a high position.

Joseph Brant was born circa 1742 in the Longhouse (meaning he was Mohawk, a descendant of the conquered Wyandot-Huron[18] through his grandmother) and a member of the Confederacy of Six Nations. In the 1750s, he was a man with feet in both the British and First Nation worlds. During the Seven Years' War, the Confederacy had sided with the British Crown and Brant saw action in the capture of Fort Frontenac (August 26–28, 1758). He joined the forces of Frederick Haldimand during the siege and capture of Fort Niagara (July 7–25, 1759), and received a medal for good conduct. The fall of Fort Niagara silenced the French forces in western New France, and, in two months time, Wolfe would close in on Quebec City.

Joseph Brant even travelled to England in 1775–76 as part of an envoy that met with the colonial secretary, Lord George Germain, and King George III to remind them of their promises of land and security for the First Nations. It was during this trip that Brant began a direct relationship with the King (and later, the Prince Regent) that would continue throughout his life. At these meetings, Brant pressed for a guarantee of First Nations' territorial claims and treaty rights. Given a captaincy in 1780, Brant fought along the western frontier, trying to stem American expansion by uniting the First Nations against them. When the British were defeated by the Americans, Captain Brant led many of the Mohawk, now Loyalists, into the Province of Quebec to settle on land bordering the Grand River (later this territory would become part of Upper Canada) promised to them by the Crown.

During a 1791 visit to Upper Canada, P. Campbell, a former officer in the 42nd Highlanders during the American Revolution, visited with Brant at his home along the Grand River near Brantford. Impressed by the Mohawk captain, Campbell wrote in his journal: "This renown warrior is not of any royal or conspicuous progenitors, but, by his ability in war and political conduct in peace, has raised himself to the highest dignity of his nation and his alliance and friendship is now courted by sovereign and foreign states."[19]

By meeting with Sir John Johnson and Joseph Brant's delegation, Prince Edward was immediately brought into their conflict with the United States. While the British Crown had made peace with the Americans in 1783, the First Nations had not, and continued to wage the Northwestern War along the western frontier (territory that would eventually become the states of Ohio, Indiana, Illinois, Michigan, and Wisconsin, as well as the northeastern part of Minnesota). Presenting themselves as allies of the Crown, the delegation also intended to bring attention to further encroachments on Native lands by the United States. Lord Dorchester officially presented Prince Edward to the First Nations by saying, "Brothers! Here is Prince Edward, son of our King, who has just arrived with a chosen band of his Warriors, to protect this Country. I leave him second in command [Lord Dorchester was about to return to England for a short visit] of all the King's Warriors in Canada, and he will also take care of you."[20]

The scene of the dozens of First Nations peoples gazing into the face of the twenty-three-year-old Prince must have been memorable. Being a "Prince of the Blood" made Edward a living link of the Covenant Chain, the treaties that bound the Crown and First Nations together in honour. No speech from Edward is recorded from this meeting as it is likely that the governor was the only one to officially speak on behalf of the King.

Dorchester's words to the assembled First Nations would eventually be quoted to President George Washington on February 26, 1793, by Colonel Josiah Parker, the member of the House of Representatives for Virginia. Colonel Parker had just delivered a speech on the Crown's support of First Nations' actions against the United States after receiving a letter from John Graves Simcoe, writing as lieutenant governor of Upper Canada, and citing Dorchester's speech. Two years after his introduction at Quebec, Edward's presence in Canada would be used by an ambitious lieutenant governor to threaten the United States with the Crown's intention to protect its First Nations allies and the lands they inhabited.[21]

Prince Edward's introduction to the rest of Quebec's high society would occur over a series of levees and other social events as the capital of the vast Province of Quebec (as the territory was then known as) prepared itself for the proclamation of the Constitution Act of 1791, which was to take place on December 26th. Once in force, the Act would separate the extensive Province of Quebec into Upper Canada (modern-day Ontario) and Lower Canada (modern-day Quebec). The city in which Edward found himself was swarming with activity.

Lord Dorchester was not in favour of the splitting of the current Quebec territory into two new political entities. For some time he had been lobbying the British government to divide Canada into four districts, each with a lieutenant governor to handle internal affairs, but ultimately deferring to a governor general. Foreshadowing Confederation by nearly a century, Dorchester insisted that Canada could only be unified under a powerful central government under the Crown, but his entreaties fell on deaf ears back in England.[22]

The Constitution Act of 1791 was largely in response to the needs of the thousands of new Loyalist settlers that poured into British North America in the wake of the American Revolution. At the time of the Royal Proclamation of 1763, the French population of what would become the Province of Quebec hovered at 78,000 habitants, but by 1791 that number had swelled to 120,000. Since the American Declaration of Independence in 1776, some 40,000 Loyalist refugees had fled north to settle in the British Province of Quebec — from Amherstburg on the Detroit River to Quebec City — with another 30,000 heading east to the provinces of Nova Scotia, New Brunswick, and St. John's Island.[23]

With only 10,000 Loyalists settling in what would become Upper Canada, the British government moved to protect what it hoped would become a thoroughly British colony from being submerged by the dominant French-speaking legislature in Quebec City. The splitting of the Province of Quebec into two distinct areas, each with its own legislative assembly, council, and lieutenant governor, allowed the Loyalists of Upper Canada to retain the British institutions they had fought to preserve, while at the same time permitting the French Canadians in Lower Canada to live under the freedoms guaranteed to them by the 1774 Quebec Act.[24] The head of the new province of Upper Canada was to be John Graves Simcoe, who had arrived with his wife aboard the *Triton* on November 11, 1791. Simcoe arrived in Quebec carrying a letter for the Prince from his father, informing him that the King would pay off the debts incurred during his posting at Gibraltar. Edward was euphoric.

"I do not remember, Sir, ever to have experienced so happy a moment as that in which I which I first saw your [*sic*] Majesty's hand writing on the superscription of this letter."[25] This small but critical affirmation from his father gave Edward the boost of confidence he needed, and he quickly assured the King that he would get his finances in order. Edward also expressed the hope that he could remain in Canada with his Royal Fusiliers until the summer of 1793, after which he wanted to be transferred to Windsor Castle (thus rejoining his family) with his regiment.

An empire builder to the core, John Graves Simcoe would have relished the opportunity to endear himself to the Prince (Simcoe must have silently patted himself on the back once the nature of the letter was revealed). An important relationship developed between Simcoe and Prince Edward, one that, while not blossoming into a close friendship, continued through correspondence until Simcoe's death in 1806. Once the Constitution Act took effect on December 26 that year, Simcoe would become

Upper Canada's first lieutenant governor, much to the conster-
nation of Lord Dorchester, who still favoured Sir John Johnson.
But the governor general would have to live with Simcoe — a
situation that would prove difficult for the two men.[26]

Born in Cotterstock, England, in 1752, John Graves Simcoe
was one of two sons born to Captain John and Katherine Simcoe.
Captain Simcoe had been commander of HMS *Pembroke* during the North American campaign of the Seven Years' War. Like
Dorchester, he supported the forces of Major-General Jeffery
Amherst and Brigadier General James Wolfe, and participated
in the 1758 siege of Louisburg. Captain Simcoe died of pneumonia as he sailed across the Gulf of St. Lawrence while escorting
transports carrying soldiers destined for the Plains of Abraham.
Watching his captain's body being buried at sea was a young
ship's master, the future navigator and explorer James Cook.

Following the death of his father, John Graves Simcoe
was educated at Eton College before being enrolled at Merton
College at Oxford. Seemingly destined to become a lawyer, he
found his path changed dramatically at the age of eighteen. On
April 27, 1770, his mother purchased a commission for him
as an ensign in the 35th Regiment of Foot. Following the purchase of another commission, Simcoe was promoted to lieutenant in 1774.

At the outbreak of the American Revolution, Simcoe was
sent to New England with the 35th Regiment. While the British
fleet, commanded by his godfather, Vice Admiral Samuel Graves
of the North American Squadron of the Royal Navy, surrounded
Boston, Simcoe landed in the city just days after the Battle of
Bunker Hill. By 1775, Simcoe had purchased a captaincy in the
40th Regiment of Foot and within two years found himself in
command of the Queen's Rangers.

Created during the Seven Years' War, the Queen's Rangers were crack guerrilla soldiers, noted for their green tunics, the first instance of camouflage being used by a modern European army. The Rangers originated from a warrant granted to American Robert Rogers to raise companies of men that could, in the words of Simcoe biographers Mary Beacock Fryer and Christopher Dracott, "operate with greater mobility than conventional infantry."[27] Blending the war tactics of the British with those of their First Nations allies, the Rangers became a force to be reckoned with, and their tactics were often viewed as questionable in the eyes of traditional generals from England. They certainly were not soldiers of the line, as explained by Fryer and Dracott:

> The first requirement for a ranger was that he be able to endure severe hardship for long periods of time, miles from the comforts of civilization.... In summer they marched or travelled in whaleboats, bateaux or canoes; in winter they used sleighs, skates or snowshoes.
>
> On scouting missions rangers walked widely spread out to prevent more than one being a target for an enemy marksman. When crossing swampy ground, they marched abreast to confound trackers. They made camp after dark on a spot where sentries would have a clear view of the enemy and not be surprised.... They were adept at setting up an ambush.[28]

Lord Dorchester knew of the Rangers' guerrilla tactics, which included border raids and scalping, and saw them as a dishonourable aspect of war in America. That Simcoe was their commanding officer was not lost on Dorchester, giving the governor another reason to distrust him.

Simcoe had assumed command of the Queen's Rangers on October 15, 1777. Almost two years later, on May 2, 1779, the Queen's Rangers became the 1st American Regiment and Simcoe was promoted to the provincial rank of lieutenant-colonel. A short time later he was taken prisoner by American rebels during a raid on New York and held for four months at Burlington, New Jersey, before being released.

As the situation grew more desperate for the British in the Thirteen Colonies, the now Colonel Simcoe began suggesting to his Rangers — most of whom were Loyalists — that they try to rejoin the American rebels, for fear of what would happen to them once the Crown surrendered. Because of his chronic ill health, a permanent state he had in common with Prince Edward, Simcoe was sent to the British stronghold of New York before the formal capitulation of British forces on October 19, 1781. Due to the limited space available, Simcoe had the wounded Rangers travel with him onboard the ship to New York to permit their evacuation back to England, but those Rangers left behind along the western frontier were not protected from the wrath of the victorious rebel forces. Some were executed as soon as they were discovered.

John Graves Simcoe was sent back to England where he would continue to lobby for his Rangers to be included on the British Regimental Lists, thus allowing them to receive pay and legitimate rank recognition (colonial ranks were not recognized back in England) — an effort that was rewarded when the "Queen's American Rangers" were added to the Army List in 1782. In late December of that year, John Graves Simcoe married Elizabeth Posthuma Gwillim of Whitchurch, Herefordshire.

Growing restless in England, Simcoe dreamed of moving to Vermont, which in the 1780s was still an independent state and seemed as if it might return to the Crown as a British province rather than join the United States. But, by the spring of 1790, it was common knowledge that Simcoe was to be appointed as the first lieutenant governor of Upper Canada. Foremost in the mind of the new representative of the King was the creation of a new British empire in the heart of North America to counter the influence of the United States. With this in mind, the future lieutenant governor wrote to Henry Dundas, the new home secretary: "There may be a distant period in which it may be possible that the Inhabitants of the Sea Coasts of Canada and on the River St. Lawrence shall conceive that an unrestrained Trade will be more beneficial to them than a dependant Connection with Great Britain — but such can never be the ideas of the Inhabitants of Upper Canada ..."[29]

Simcoe's vision for his new province flew in the face of Lord Dorchester's plan for a united colony under a powerful governor general, largely because of the suggestion that there be co-equal representatives of the Crown, and that the lieutenant governor of Upper Canada was to be master of his domain and not subject to a higher representative of the Crown. In many ways, Simcoe's vision of the Crown in British North America foreshadows the modern provincial-federal "Compound Monarchy"[30] that exists in Canada today.

Unable to be sworn in as lieutenant governor until three of the members selected for his executive council were present (two of them — Chief Justice William Osgoode and Receiver General Peter Russell — were still in England), a frustrated Simcoe had to wait out the winter in Quebec City. During the long cold months the future lieutenant governor set about lobbying for a promotion to the rank of major general so that he would not be outranked by his peers. It irked Simcoe that the soldiers stationed in Upper Canada would automatically defer to Sir John Johnson, Sir Alured Clarke (both held the rank of brigadier general), and Prince Edward (a colonel with the Royal Fusiliers).

In a letter to Henry Dundas, dated September 6, 1791, written before departing for North America, Simcoe complained:

> Apprehending that His Majesty is not inclined to give me the Appointment of Brigadier General in America, (which I was promised,) in consequence of the Senior Rank which His Royal Highness Prince Edward has ever held as Colonel.... It was therefore long after my destination to the Appointment of Upper Canada when I understood that Prince Edward was ordered to Quebec, I *foresaw at once* the Impropriety of the Rank which I was to hold being given to me ...[31]

The day after his arrival in Quebec, Simcoe issued a private letter to his friend Sir George Yonge, the British secretary of war, lamenting his rank in relation to Prince Edward. Ultimately, his efforts paid off, and Simcoe would be promoted to full colonel in Britain on November 18, 1791 (the day after he sent yet another plea to Henry Dundas from Quebec), although he would not learn of his promotion until the following spring.

While Simcoe found his wait in Quebec tedious, his wife did not. Elizabeth Simcoe threw herself into the ongoing balls, concerts, dinners, and winter festivities celebrated in French Canada, many of which were hosted, as well as funded, by the

Prince. During these events she became well-acquainted with Prince Edward, and spent many evenings dancing with the King's son, and spending time with his French mistress. Undoubtedly, Elizabeth's husband was there, possibly trying to strengthen his political position and maybe even grumbling in the corner about being trapped in Quebec when he should be governing his new province. Interestingly, there is no mention of his ever dancing in Elizabeth's diary.

Elizabeth Posthuma Simcoe would play a significant role in early Upper Canadian history. A prolific diarist, painter, and adventurer, she was well-educated, being fluent in both French and German, and endowed with an inquisitive mind. Born in Whitchurch, Herefordshire, in 1766, she lost her mother, Elizabeth Spinckes Gwillim, during childbirth. Her father, Thomas Gwillim, who had served as an aide-de-camp to General Wolfe in Quebec, had been killed seven months earlier; hence Elizabeth was raised

Archives Ontario, F 47-11-1-0-18.

Elizabeth Simcoe's drawings detailing an officer's (top) and Canadian's (bottom) winter carriage in Quebec, circa 1792.

by her maternal aunt, Margaret Spinckes. When Elizabeth was six years old, her aunt married Admiral Samuel Graves, who, as noted earlier, was godfather to John Graves Simcoe. It was through this connection that John and Elizabeth Simcoe were ultimately matched.

Initially underwhelmed by the cold greyness of Quebec, Elizabeth Simcoe warmed to the society that had quickly gathered around Prince Edward and Julie de St. Laurent. Her famous diary is filled with references to great concerts and dances held at the Royal Fusiliers' barracks, as well as forays into the surrounding region with the Prince. Her entry for December 5, 1791, reads:

> A thaw today; the air Raw and cold, and the roads full of Cahots,[32] but it did not deter the Prince & a Party from driving 8 miles to Lorette. It is the custom here to make parties to dine in the Country at a distance of 10 miles. They often carry a cold dinner & return to a dance in the Evening & this in the severest weather which seems as much relished by the English as the Canadians.[33]

Prince Edward had settled in with Julie in the Upper Town of Quebec at 6 St. Louis Street. In all probability, Julie de St. Laurent was with him during most of his appearances at local parties, dances, and concerts, although she had no official role during state ceremonies and other governmental affairs. Amateur historian Jean Donald Gow, however, does offer a quotation from the Prince that challenges the assumption that de St. Laurent had no official role, but fails to offer a source to verify it: "Madame de St. Laurent … presides at my table, goes everywhere into company with me, and it is a rule with me never to accept of an invitation where there are ladies, unless she is asked …"[34]

In addition to responsibilities related to regimental life, the Prince travelled throughout the region, even renting a villa built by Governor Haldimand at the top of Montmorency Falls, east of Quebec City.[35] Edward distributed good-conduct medals to deserving soldiers posted to Lower Canada, and entertained the community with the regimental band he had brought to the city at his own tremendous expense. The Prince's regiment even put on amateur plays for the local residents of Quebec (Elizabeth Simcoe records her husband as being offended by these performances, mumbling that acting was beneath officers, and refusing to attend — she did not share her husband's beliefs on the subject).

It is around this time that stories of Edward's affairs begin to emerge in Canadian mythology, being reproduced in popular histories and articles. Today, many individuals claim they are descendants of Prince Edward Augustus, thanks to the number of offspring he allegedly fathered with Julie, as well as a string of lovers he entertained while he lived on the continent.[36]

The stories and gossip that the Crown affords the society in which it exists are an important aspect of society, then as now. Magnified by its position at the heart of society, the lore (irrespective of whether it is true or not) of the Royal family members reflects the culture in which they exist. It is true that their personal lives are windows into the goings on of high society, and the public's thirst for such stories is voracious. The length of Edward's relationship with Julie has fascinated people since the couple met in Gibraltar, leading to all kinds of incredible tales.

While Edward was not completely faithful to his mistress during their twenty-seven years together, stories of an overly pious Prince (by twenty-first-century standards) are false. Publicly, the Prince was completely devoted to Madame de St. Laurent, but at the same time he also paid private visits to known prostitutes — a common practice by members of "high society." Such visits may have been one of the reasons Edward's mother and sisters referred to him as "Joseph Surface," the hypocritical womanizer and social climber in Richard Brinsley Sheridan's *The School for Scandal* (first performed in London in 1777).

Still, the many tales of numerous illegitimate children attached to Edward and Julie de St. Laurent, or to Edward's lovers such as Eliza Green (with whom he did have a sexual relationship) appear to be fabrications. Author Mollie Gillen convincingly argues that no Canadian children were born to the Prince.[37]

The Quebec residence of Prince Edward Augustus on 6 St. Louis Street. The building is now occupied by the French Consulate.

On the religious side, Prince Edward was known for being sympathetic to Roman Catholics back in England, and, during his time in Quebec, he seemed to prefer the company of French Canadians. Jean Donald Gow penned comments into the margins of her final manuscript purporting that Edward had a common touch that appealed to French, Loyalists, and American farmers.[38] The Prince established meaningful relationships with prominent Catholic families in Lower Canada — most notably Seigneur Ignace-Michel-Louis-Antoine "Louis" d'Irumberry de Salaberry and his family, whose village was on the road to the Montmorency Falls. Their relationship would continue, through a rich correspondence, after Edward returned to England, until the Prince's death in 1820.

Louis de Salaberry was a member of the legislative assembly for the old Province of Quebec, and his family had roots that took them back to Basque country in Europe. Before the French Revolution, Louis had been presented to King Louis XVI, kissed the hand of Queen Marie Antoinette, and watched the Dauphin play in the Tuileries Palace. The friendship between Prince Edward and the de Salaberrys became so close that when a son was born to Louis and his wife, Françoise-Catherine, on July 2, 1792, the infant was christened Édouard-Alphonse after both his royal godfather and Julie (Julie's official name was "Madame Alphonsine Julie Thérèse Bernardine de Montgenêt, Baronne de Fortisson").

A problem had emerged around the actual christening since the de Salaberrys were Roman Catholic and the Prince was son of the defender of the Protestant Church of England. Edward was quick to remind the Catholic Church in Canada of its precarious position in the country, assuring the de Salaberrys that he would be godfather not as the son of the King, but rather as son of a Sovereign who had given special protection to the Roman Catholic clergy in Canada.[39] Ultimately, the Catholic bishop of Quebec, Jean-François Hubert, diplomatically circumvented the issue as explained in a letter addressed to King George III:

> [A]t the actual baptism ceremony the village priest, Father Renauld [parish of Maskinongé], held the child and in prearranged words of no ambiguity the Bishop [Charles-François Bailly de Messein] said: "This child is born a Catholic; he is to be baptized as a child of the Catholic Church, Apostolic and Roman; Monseigneur, what name does Your Highness give to this child?" "Édouard," said the Prince, and Father Renaud offered the child to the Bishop for naming; in this way The Prince is not really the godfather. It is Monseigneur de Capse.[40]

As planned, on December 26, 1791, Lord Dorchester proclaimed the Constitution Act and the political division of Upper Canada and Lower Canada was formalized. Elizabeth Simcoe noted the event succinctly in her diary: "This day the Division of the Province into Upper & Lower Canada & the new Constitution given to the former was announced by Proclamation. There were dinners at the Hotels & illuminations at night to commemorate this event."[41] Two days later a ball was held at the Château Saint-Louis and Prince Edward danced with the elites of his father's two new provinces. Earlier the same day, the merchants of the Lower Town of Quebec had waited on the merchants of the Upper Town at Frank's Tavern, proposing and drinking twenty-three toasts in honour of the new constitution.

As for John Graves Simcoe, his attention was now immediately focused on his new appointment. All that needed to happen now was the arrival of members of his executive from England so that he could be officially sworn in as lieutenant governor. In the meantime, another string of royal balls and regimental dinners would have to suffice, as tedious as he may have found them. It also may have been during this period of waiting that Simcoe approached Prince Edward about undertaking a royal tour of Upper Canada during the upcoming summer. Certainly the presence of the Prince in the new province would fit the image that the lieutenant governor had for the region.

Over the next few months officials organized themselves into two separate governments in Canada. One of their first orders of business was to fill the new legislatures, so elections were ordered for the upcoming spring and summer of 1792.

Thus, it was that on June 27 Louis de Salaberry found himself running for a seat in the legislative assembly of Lower Canada in the nearby settlement of Charlesbourg. With de Salaberry in the lead (the voting stood at Louis de Salaberry, 515; David Lynd, 462; Berthelot Dartigny, 436), the poll was ordered closed after an hour had passed with no new voters arriving (the law at the time stated that two candidates could demand a poll closed if an hour passed without a new voter showing up). Shortly after the poll was declared closed, however, candidate Berthelot Dartigny appeared with sixty-two supporters from the area, all demanding to vote. The demonstration turned violent, splitting along French-English lines as the unruly crowd pulled down the building that housed the polling station. Hearing of the violence, Prince Edward hurriedly left Quebec City and headed for the scene of the riot at Charlesbourg, roughly seven and a half miles away. Dr. William James Anderson, a Scottish doctor who had settled in Quebec in 1860 and became president of the Quebec Literary and Historical Society, wrote about the event in his 1870 biography of the Prince:

> Prince Edward hearing of it, hastened to Charlebourg, and thus addressed the rioters, in French: "Can there be a man among you who does not take the King to be the father of his people? Is there a man among you who does not look upon the new constitution as the best possible one both for the subject and the Government? Part then in peace; I urge you to unanimity and concord. Let me hear no more of the odious distinctions of French and English. *You are all* his Britannic Majesty's Canadian subjects." The tumult ceased, and gave place to admiration and applause.[42]

Edward's statement is significant for two reasons: Firstly, the Prince employed the Crown as a great unifier, an umbrella for the separate cultures that were now forced to co-exist in Canada. Secondly, Edward used the term "Canadian" to refer to both the French and English inhabitants of the country. According to Canadian royal historians Arthur Bousfield and Gary Toffoli, this is the first recorded use of this term, in this way.

In a society searching for common ground and identity, whether knowingly or not, the young prince had reinforced the institution of the Crown as a great scaffolding within which modern Canada could emerge. Bousfield and Toffoli write in *Home to Canada: Royal Tour, 1786–2010* that Edward redefined "Canadian" to include both English and French as inhabitants of the country and giving the term its modern meaning. Coming from the King's own son, the new sense of the word carried authority.[43] Prince Edward's use of "Canadian" was a huge step in the establishment of the country's national identity as a bilingual, and even multicultural (as the term would later be expanded to include many different ethnic groups) state.

As to the circumstances of the riot in Charlebourg, Jonathan Sewell later wrote to fellow lawyer Ward Chipman in Fredericton, New Brunswick, that some in the mob "attempted by every means & pitiful artifice to keep alive that odious distinction of French & English," with some even threatening violence on the Prince.[44] But, by appealing to the unity inspired by the Crown and the new nationality being created within it, Prince Edward was ultimately able to calm the crowd.[45]

Edward's first year in Canada saw him effectively present himself as an instrument of unity and a capable ambassador for the King. Together, he and Julie brought a cosmopolitan air to the levees and regimental balls being thrown in Quebec City in honour of the birth of a new Canada with the proclamation of the Constitution Act of 1791. He also presented himself as a unifier for the fractious relationship that existed between the English and French inhabitants of the province. Both cultural groups were "Canadian" in the eyes of the Prince, united in loyalty with the First Nations allies of the country. Edward's visit to Upper Canada, concocted over the winter with John Graves Simcoe, however, would present a much different image. Simcoe's vision for his new province was as a centre for a new British empire — totally Anglocentric in its very concept.

The Prince would soon be pulled in two very different directions by two distinct images of Canada by the summer of 1792. On the one hand, Edward had befriended many prominent French Canadians (this is especially true of the de Salaberrys), enjoying their company and acceptance of Madame de St. Laurent. Edward spoke French fluently, allowing himself to be immersed in the culture of Canada's original European inhabitants. For the Prince, Canada was overwhelmingly French. Travelling west, however, Edward would notice the tension created by the immigration of thousands of American Loyalists into Lower Canada. In Upper Canada, a completely different narrative was being created. Any French traces were intentionally being eradicated by a lieutenant governor bent on creating a new British nation to counter the United States.

The First Nations peoples (both Loyalists and indigenous) were becoming increasing lost in the tug-of-war for the future of British North America. For them, Edward was a living link to the Covenant Chain between King George and their elders. His presence continued alliances built through treaties with a far-off King that many First Nations saw as their only hope in retaining or regaining their land rights. At the same time, the long Canadian winter, while easier on his health, and despite the many social occasions, had only increased Edward's sense of isolation from his family.

The Prince was homesick.

4

The 1792 Royal Tour of Upper Canada

John Graves Simcoe had a vision for the new province of Upper Canada, and, by June 8, 1792, the newly appointed lieutenant governor and his wife Elizabeth headed up the St. Lawrence River from Quebec to see it carried out. Within two months of the arrival of the Simcoes, Upper Canada would host its first Royal Tour, and Prince Edward Augustus' visit reflected the foundations being laid by the new lieutenant governor across the region.

Before departing England, John Graves Simcoe had a clear idea of the future of Upper Canada and was willing to share that vision with whoever would listen (this undoubtedly included Prince Edward during their winter together in Quebec). Simcoe saw the great peninsula framed by lakes Erie, Huron, and Ontario (called "The Great Peninsular Region") as the natural homeland of a new British Nation at the very heart of North America. In a letter to Sir Joseph Banks,[1] Simcoe

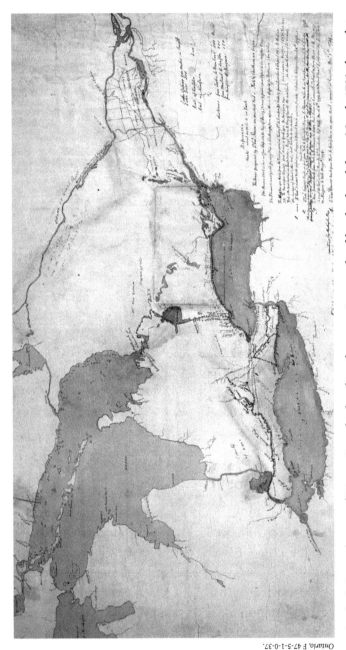

Elizabeth Simcoe's map of Upper Canada detailing the extensive travels of her husband from March 1793 through to September 1795. Note that forts Detroit, Niagara, Michilimackinac, and Oswego are still included as British military installations.

wrote: "For the purpose of commerce, union, and power, I propose that the site of the colony should be in that Great Peninsula
between the Lakes Huron, Erie, and Ontario, a spot destined by
nature, sooner or later, to govern the interior world."[2]

For Simcoe, the establishment of Upper Canada was a new
development in the battle against American republicanism.
Unable to defeat the former British colonies by force, the lieutenant governor hoped that the establishment of a "free, honourable
British Government, and a pure administration of its laws ..."[3]
would present to the Americans a style of freedom that was no
longer possible now that they had broken from the Crown. Simcoe
believed that waves of immigrants would pour into the colony
from desperate Loyalists still remaining in the United States —
particularly those from Connecticut and Vermont. The new representative of the King was emphatic that there were thousands of
oppressed American Loyalists who could be enticed north with
the promise of sound British government — as well as cheap land
— under the Crown, and he had solid reasons for his beliefs.

Simcoe's plans tapped into the fact that the republican
form of government created out of the American Revolution
(uniting a fractious collection of independent states) was
not as firmly entrenched as many believed. American
Founding Father Alexander Hamilton's[4] notes from the 1787
Constitutional Convention held in Philadelphia[5] include his
belief that the British Constitution, including its monarchy,
was the best form of government, providing a better chance
for good administration.[6] James Madison (a political rival and
future president of the United States) wrote that Hamilton
even mused about an elective monarchy during the debates of
what the American executive should look like, leading many to
label him as a monarchist. Thomas Jefferson — another future

A PROCLAMATION,

To fuch as are defirous to fettle on the lands of the crown in the Province of

UPPER CANADA;

BY HIS EXCELLENCY

John Graves Simcoe, Efquire;

Lieutenant Governor and Commander in Chief of the faid Province, and Colonel
Commanding His Majefty's Forces, &c. &c. &c.

BE IT KNOWN to all concerned, that his majefty hath, by his royal commiffion and inftructions to the governor, and in his abfence the lieutenant governor or perfon adminiftering the government for the time being, of the faid Province of Upper Canada, given authority and command to grant the lands of the crown in the fame by patent under the great feal thereof ; and it being expedient to publifh and declare the royal intention refpecting fuch grants and patents, I do accordingly hereby make known the terms of grant and fettlement to be :

First.—That the crown lands to be granted be parcel of townfhip : if an inland townfhip, of ten miles fquare, and if a townfhip on navigable waters, of nine miles in front and twelve miles in depth, be run out and marked by his majefty's furveyor or deputy furveyor general, or under his fanction and authority.

Second.—That only fuch part of the townfhip be granted as fhall remain, after a refervation of one feventh part thereof, for the fupport of a proteftant clergy, and one other feventh part thereof, for the future difpofition of the crown.

Third.—That no farm lot fhall be granted to any one perfon which fhall contain more than two hundred acres ; yet the governor, lieutenant governor or perfon adminiftering the government, is allowed and permitted to grant to any perfon or perfons fuch further quantity of land as they may defire, not exceeding one thoufand acres, over and above what may have been before granted to them.

Fourth.—That every petitioner for lands make it appear, that he or fhe is in a condition to cultivate and improve the fame, and fhall, befides taking the ufual oaths, fubfcribe a declaration (before proper perfons to be for that purpofe appointed) of the tenor of the words following, viz. " I A. B. do promife and declare that I will maintain and defend to the utmoft of my power the authority of the king in his parliament as the fupreme legiflature of this Province.'

Fifth.—That applications for grants be made by petition to the governor, lieutenant governor, or perfon adminiftering the government for the time being, & where it is advifeable to grant the prayer thereof a warrant fhall iffue to the proper officer for a furvey thereof, returnable within fix months with a plot annexed, and be followed with a patent granting the fame, if defired, in free and common foccage, upon the terms and conditions in the royal inftructions expreffed, and herein after fuggefted.

Sixth.—That all grants referve to the crown, all coals, commonly called fea coals, and mines of gold, filver, copper, tin, iron, and lead ; and each patent contain a claufe for the refervation of timber for the royal navy of the tenor following : ' And provided alfo, that no part of the tract or parcel of land hereby granted to the faid _____ and his heirs, be within any refervation heretofore made and ' by us, our heirs and fucceffors, by our furveyor general of woods, or his lawful deputy ; in ' which cafe, this our grant for fuch part of the land hereby given and granted to the faid ' and his heirs forever as aforefaid, and which fhall upon furvey thereof being made, be found within ' any fuch refervation, fhall be null and void, any thing herein contained to the contrary notwithftanding.'

Seventh.—That the two feventh referved for the crown's future difpofition, and the fupport of a proteftant clergy, be not fevered tracts, each of one feventh part of the townfhip, but fuch lots or farms therein, as the furveyor-general's return of the furvey of the townfhip, fhall be defcribed as fet apart for thefe purpofes, between the other farms of which the faid townfhip fhall confift, to the intent that the lands to be referved may be nearly of the like value with an equal quantity of the other parts to be granted out as afore-mentioned.

Eighth.—That the refpective patentees are to take the eftates granted to them feverally free of quit rent and of any other expences, than fuch fees as are or may be allowed to be demanded and received by the different officers concerned in paffing the patent and recording the fame, to be ftated in a table authorized and eftablifhed by the government, and publickly fixed up in the feveral offices of the clerk of the council, of the furveyor general, and of the fecretary of the Province.

Ninth.—That every patent be entered upon record within fix months from the date thereof, in the fecretary's or regifter's offices, and a docket thereof in the auditor's office.

Tenth.—Whenever it fhall be thought advifeable to grant any given quantity to one perfon of one thoufand acres or under, and the fame cannot be found by reafon of the faid refervations and prior grants within the townfhip in the petition expreffed, the fame, or what fhall be requifite to make up to fuch perfon the quantity advifed, fhall be located to him, in fome other townfhip, upon a new petition for that purpofe to be preferred.

And of the faid feveral regulations, all perfons concerned are to take notice, and govern themfelves accordingly.

Given under my hand and feal, in the city of Quebec, the feventh day of February, in the thirty-fecond year of his majefty's reign, and in the year of our Lord, one thoufand, feven hundred and ninety-two.

John Graves Simcoe.

BY HIS EXCELLENCY's COMMAND,

THOMAS TALBOT, *Acting Secretary.*

Re-printed at *Newark, by* G. Tiffany, 1795.

Proclamation by Lieutenant Governor John Graves Simcoe outlining the guidelines for the settlement of Upper Canada, a 1795 reproduction printed in Newark (Niagara-on-the-Lake). Simcoe issued this proclamation on February 7, 1792, while he was still in Quebec.

president — wrote in his notes on November 11, 1792, that Hamilton had been heard to declare that "there was no stability no security in any kind of government but a monarchy" during a dinner with colleagues.[7]

Hamilton's beliefs reflect growing concerns in the American republic around the balance between state and federal governments. Many saw the Crown as the only institution that could promote the necessary executive and unity needed in order to keep the United States from flying apart at its seams — indeed, this would happen less than a century later with the American Civil War (1861–65), a conflict that prompted the Canadian Fathers of Confederation to pay close attention to the relationships between the provinces and Ottawa.[8]

Even President George Washington was aware that the United States could slip back into a monarchy. In one of the unpublished drafts for his inauguration speech the reluctant first president pointed to the fact that he lacked an immediate heir, and thus had no intention to become a monarch: "[T]he Divine Providence hath not seen fit, that my blood should be transmitted or my name perpetuated by the endearing, though sometimes seducing channel of immediate offspring. I have no child for whom I could wish to make a provision — no family to build in greatness upon my country's ruins."[9]

During the year of Prince Edward's Royal Tour to Upper Canada, Alexander Hamilton wrote an extensive letter to his friend Edward Carrington[10] detailing his distrust of James Madison and Thomas Jefferson (who, coincidentally, on the day Simcoe left Quebec for Upper Canada wrote, "[There are heads] among us itching for crowns, coronets, and mitr[es, but I hope] we sooner cut them off than gratify their [itching][11]). Emphasizing his strong attachment to the American republic, Hamilton goes on to deflect any attention on his own musings for an American Crown by saying he believed Jefferson and Madison were both surrounded by individuals with monarchist leanings.[12]

In the fall of 1792, Thomas Jefferson met with George Washington at Mount Vernon, countering the president's assertion that there were not ten men in his country who entertained a thought of returning to a monarchy. Identifying Alexander Hamilton as a monarchist, Jefferson told his president, "there was a numerous sect who had monarchy in contemplation," quoting Hamilton as saying "this [American] constitution was a shilly shally thing of mere milk and water, and was only a step to something better."[13]

Such news had travelled to Simcoe, and the lieutenant governor was keenly aware of the active monarchist sentiment in the United States. On the eve of Prince Edward's visit to Newark, Simcoe wrote to the lieutenant governor of Lower Canada, Alured Clarke:

> Should Congress adopt a Prince of the House of Brunswick [George III's royal house] for their future President or King, the happiness of the two Nations would be interwoven and united, all jealousies removed, and the most desirable affections cemented, that perhaps were formed between two Nations. This is an object worthy [of] the attention of Great Britain, and which many of the most temperate men of the United States have in contemplation, and which many events, if once systematically begun, may hasten and bring to maturity.[14]

Simcoe does not identify which Prince of the House of Brunswick he meant, although there were discussions around inviting Prince Frederick Augustus (second son of King George III), or even Prince Henry of Prussia to assume an American throne.

Even though the United States was not destined to become a constitutional monarchy, many of Britain's royal vestiges persisted. As Edward journeyed across Lake Ontario, a debate existed in the republic as to how President George Washington would be properly addressed by his fellow Americans. All kinds of submissions were made, including "His Excellency," "His Most Serene Highness," "High Mightness" (this was the president's preference), "His Elective Majesty," and "His Highness the President of the United States of America and Protector of the Rights of the Same." During the first session of Congress an idea was even put forward to have a throne placed in the Senate for Washington to sit upon.[15]

Feeding off of such monarchist feelings in the former Thirteen Colonies, John Graves Simcoe set about creating Upper Canada as an ultra-British territory (the lieutenant governor was prolific in his naming of landmarks, whitewashing the landscape of its previous First Nations and French nomenclatures: Niagara became Newark, La Tranche became the Thames River, and so on). Simcoe envisioned an Anglican bishop specifically appointed to the region, as well as an English chief justice. The King's representative also had plans for the development of the arts and education of the region as explained in his letter to Sir Joseph Banks:

> [Y]ou will see how highly important it will be, that this colony, (which I mean to show forth with all the advantages of British protection as a better Government than the United States can possibly obtain) should in its very foundations

provide for every assistance that can possibly be procured for the arts and sciences, and for every embellishment that hereafter may decorate and attract notice, and may point it out to the neighbouring States as a superior, more happy, and more polished form of Government.[16]

Public libraries, universities, importing plant species such as flax and hemp, as well as the foundation of a society (perhaps in the image of London's Royal Society) were all in Simcoe's plans for the new colony — including a new capital named Georgina planted in the very heart of the peninsula.[17] In a letter to Henry Dundas (British secretary of state) one week before the vice-regal party departed Quebec for Montreal and the frontier, Simcoe was clear that his plans for the great peninsula had not faded since his crossing to North America or his winter in Quebec:

[T]he utmost attention should be paid that British Customs, Manners and Principals, in the most trivial, as well as serious matters should be promoted and inculcated, to obtain their due ascendancy, to assimilate the Colony with its Parent State, and to bear insensibly all their habitual Influence in the support of that British Constitution, which has been so wisely extended to that Country.[18]

This was not a vision to be implemented in the distant future; rather, the lieutenant governor underscored that it needed to take place immediately.[19]

This was the political climate that Prince Edward Augustus (and probably Julie de St. Laurent) found themselves in after traversing the cascades at the confluence of the Ottawa and St. Lawrence Rivers. Once the Prince's royal barge cruised past the seigneury of Longueuil (the last of the seigneuries), opposite the southern edge of Montreal, it entered a land in the process of being reinvented.

Since the end of the hostilities of the American Revolutionary War, the northern coastline of Lake Ontario had become dotted with makeshift refugee camps inhabited by displaced American Loyalists. By 1792, the original tents and crude log cabins had evolved into small settlements, surrounded by quickly surveyed townships. Edward's royal barge floated down the St. Lawrence, following the shorelines of the 1784 "Royal Townships." Originally only numbered, the townships were named in 1788 after the members of the Royal family (Lancaster, Charlottenburgh, Cornwall, Osnabruck, Williamsburgh, Matilda, Edwardsburgh, Augusta and Elizabethtown, Kingston, Ernestown, Fredericksburgh, Adolphustown, and Marysburgh).

Arriving in the township of Cornwall, Edward's party stayed at "Maple Grove," the home of Loyalist Jeremiah French (representative of the Eastern District in the newly formed parliament).[20] The French family tell of a turkey shoot that was organized for the Prince that ended tragically when Jeremiah accidentally shot and killed his daughter in front of the Royal party.

Leaving Cornwall for the open waters of Lake Ontario, the royal barge landed at Kingston in the Cataraqui region — near a great headland that Lieutenant Governor Simcoe had just christened Prince Edward County on July 16. Founded as a trading post in 1673 by Louis de Buade, Comte de Frontenac (governor general of New France), Kingston already had a long connection with both the French and British Crowns. Rene-Robert Cavelier, Sieur de La Salle, founded Fort Frontenac two years later, creating a military centre for New France until it was demolished by British forces in 1758. In anticipation of a wave of Loyalist emigration following the defeat of Crown forces during the American Revolution, Major John Ross of the 2nd Battalion, the King's Royal Regiment of New York, was sent to rebuild Fort Frontenac and prepare the region for settlement. Mills were constructed as lands were purchased from the indigenous Mississauga First Nation.

It was Captain Michael Grass who led the first group of Loyalists to the Cataraqui region, ultimately settling in Township No.1 (eventually named "King's Town" or "Kingston" after King George III). Two of the first people granted lots in Kingston were Captain Joseph Brant and his sister Molly, but the Mohawk leader eventually moved to the Grand River region.[21]

Included in the first wave of settlers to Kingston was Reverend John Stuart, D.D., who was the bishop of Nova Scotia and Quebec's official, or commissary, from 1789 to 1811. Stuart had been a missionary to the Mohawks and had fallen under the patronage of Sir John Johnson, becoming chaplain of the 2nd Battalion of the Royal Regiment of New York. Leaving New York during the Revolution, Stuart arrived in Montreal in 1781. Eventually fixing his mission at Kingston, Reverend Stuart began keeping a church registry in 1785, and built a small wood-framed church (christened St. George's) in 1792.

It was at Stuart's little church that John Graves Simcoe and his executive were first sworn in on July 8 of that year. The lieutenant governor then travelled to his temporary capital at Newark, arriving there barely one month before Edward and his entourage. Interestingly, and implying a friendship between the two that may have originated during his visit to Kingston, Prince

Edward, in his later capacity as commander-in-chief, ordered that Reverend John Stuart's chaplaincy be carried on indefinitely (despite Edward's usual trend to leave such appointments up to the discretion of the commanding officers).

A letter from Reverend Stuart survives from the vice-regal visit to Kingston by the Simcoes. Stuart, newly returned from Schenectady, New York, wrote, "I found the Governor here, on my arrival but not my friend Sir John Johnson — He has quitted this Country in Disgust [perhaps never to return] and left 99/100 of the Inhabitants of these new Settlements to lament the Loss of a Patron, Guard & Friend." Stuart goes on to note, "The Governor has brought Friends enough with him to fill all the lucrative Offices in his, or Government's Gift."[22] What upset Sir John enough to cause him to leave before the arrival of the Prince is not mentioned, but it was no secret that he had been hurt by the British government's veto of his appointment as lieutenant governor. Many existing accounts speak to the fact that Johnson and Simcoe did not get along, especially since the former reported directly to Lord Dorchester and not the lieutenant governor.

Recently, oral traditions and written documents have been uncovered, shedding light on the controversial "Gun Shot Treaty of 1792" concluded between Simcoe and various First Nations assembled at Kingston during that first vice-regal visit. Since Johnson was not under the jurisdiction of Simcoe's government in Upper Canada, he may have felt the treaty was a useless exercise by a lieutenant governor trying to assert his control over an area constitutionally outside of his authority. The 1927 Miskokomon paper describes thousands of First Nations peoples present at the negotiations, including the principal chiefs of the different tribes. Simcoe stated that even though the government wanted the land, it was not intended that the fish and game rights be included, or that the First Nations were to be deprived of their privileges of hunting, trapping, and fishing, as they were the source of their living and sustenance. The paper goes into greater detail, stating:

> These provisions were to hold good as long as the grass grows and water runs, and as long as the British Gov't is in existence [and that] According to the ruling of the Shot Gun Treaty, the Indians have first rights to all creeks, rivers and lakes, 16 feet on both sides of the said creek, 66 feet on both sides of all rivers and 99 feet around all lakes and island[s] on said lakes. This land mentioned is their inheritance ... no white man can order them off.[23]

For the remainder of his time as lieutenant governor, Simcoe lobbied the British government to have a superintendent of Indian affairs for Upper Canada who reported directly to him and not Johnson or Dorchester. Such an office would be created in 1796 after Simcoe had already left the province.

Thanks to the break away from the Crown, American states no longer had to observe the boundaries set by the Royal Proclamation of 1763 that limited westward expansion to the Appalachian Mountains. Consequently, the original populations of the Thirteen Colonies now rapidly spilled beyond their original boundaries. In 1790, the population of the United States stood at 3.9 million, most of whom lived within fifty miles of the Atlantic Ocean. By 1830 the American population had grown to twelve million, 4.5 million of whom lived west of the Appalachians. In 1820, 120,000 First Nations peoples lived east of the Mississippi River; nearly a quarter century later their population stood at less than 30,000.[24] The northwestern wars raged on, and even though Thomas Jefferson had once said that First Nations living within state boundaries should not be forced to leave, the constant influx of non-Native settlers would change his tune, particularly when he became president in 1800.

The success of Upper Canada — and British North America as a whole — depended on a treaty relationship between the Crown and First Nations. The added complexity of the Loyalist First Nations represented by Sir John Johnson (people such as the Six Nations who emigrated north from their traditional homelands in New York State so that they could remain loyal to the Crown) added another layer of negotiations. In many cases, the traditional peoples of the northern Lake Ontario shoreline (Mississauga First Nation) were being displaced by their traditional enemies (Mohawk and other Six Nations Peoples) as the Crown rewarded the later for their loyalty against the Americans, a loyalty that they would need to call on in the future if Upper and Lower Canada were to survive.

Even after the Treaty of Paris made peace between the Crown and its former American subjects, the Six Nations, allied with a number of other First Nations, continued to fight as the United States threatened expansion northwest of the Appalachian Mountains in violation of the Royal Proclamation of 1763. Both the British and Americans wanted an end to the northwestern wars along the frontier, but favoured radically different approaches. Britain wanted the establishment of a Native buffer state between their former Thirteen Colonies and Upper and Lower Canada, while the Americans saw themselves as destined to expand west unencumbered. This difference of opinion is emphasized in President George Washington's response, earlier in 1792, to a letter written by the American minister plenipotentiary to France, Gouverneur Morris, reporting that Henry Dundas had been heard saying that the Americans had requested British mediation in their conflict with the First Nations:

> You may be *fully* assured, Sir, that such *mediation* was *never* asked, that the asking of it was *never* in contemplation, and I think that I might go further and say, that it not only never *will* be asked, but would be rejected if offered. The United States will never have occasion, I hope, to ask for the interposition of that power, or any other, to establish peace within their own territory.[25]

Both First Nations (Loyalist and otherwise) and the British needed each other if they were to survive in Upper and Lower Canada — alliances that would prove vital during the War of 1812.

At the same time, the Loyalist settlers clung tenaciously to life on the shorelines of lakes Ontario and Erie, their settlements open to invasion by a hungry American army. The Crown's representatives had to walk a narrow line between appearing neutral to the eyes of the Americans, yet remain supportive to their First Nations allies. Lieutenant Governor Simcoe wrote about George Washington to Sir George Yonge (British secretary of war and expert on Roman roads),[26] just before entering his new province, saying, "I think worst of his heart than his head, and fear he will urge us into war to support his power," adding, "if we are forced into war while I govern Upper Canada, it shall not be the wisest sort, preventative war, but absolutely and entirely defensive ..."[27]

Echoing this belief, the lieutenant governor wrote to Alexander McKee (an agent in the British Indian Department) after the departure of Prince Edward, emphasizing that any appeals for British mediation in American and First Nation conflicts (already completely rejected by President Washington) must never compromise the British Crown's neutrality and that "it is neither the interest nor the intention of His Majesty's Government to commence offensive hostilities against the United States."[28]

All of these issues were swirling in the air as Prince Edward landed at Kingston in the summer of 1792. The settlement that greeted the Prince was described by Elizabeth Simcoe one month earlier as "a small Town of about fifty wooden Houses & Merchant's Store Houses. Only one House is built of stone, it belongs to a merchant. There is a small Garrison here & a harbour for ships."[29] After visiting with the local garrison and other dignitaries, Edward boarded the 80-ton schooner *Onondaga*[30] at Kingston harbour to continue across Lake Ontario to the provisional capital at Newark.

The Prince's royal progress across the great lake would have galvanized the Loyalists living along its edge. These first settlers to Upper Canada moved north out of loyalty to King George III and the "English Constitution," and had yet to be submerged by the late Loyalists — those who emigrated more for the cheap and abundant land than any attachment to the monarchy. That the son of George III was touring their region within six years of their arrival would have further reinforced their belief in the unity of the British Empire. Edward must have believed this as well, since such royal progresses were a hallmark of his time in North America.

Demonstrating his belief in the Crown as a great unifier of Canadian society, the Prince proudly wrote back to his father that he had:

[v]isited every post occupied by even the small-
est detachment of your troops throughout all
Canada, except Michillimakinac, Detroit and
Oswego. This latter place I was prevented from
seeing by a violent storm which overtook us in
our passage across Lake Ontario, and thus rendered it a matter of utter impossibility for me to
reach the fort. I had the satisfaction during my
tour of seeing every regiment, except the 24th,
now in Canada, having met the Queen's Rangers,
and the 5th Regiment at Niagara....[31]

Looking at a report prepared by Francis Le Maistre (military
secretary to Lord Dorchester), the locations and regiments visited
by Prince Edward during his Royal Tour from Quebec to Newark
would have included:[32]

Regiments	Locations
5th Regiment of Foot	Upper Canada: Fort Erie Disputed Territory: Fort Niagara, Fort Schlosser
26th Regiment of Foot	Lower Canada: Fort Chambly, Fort St. Johns (Jean), Île aux Noix, Point au Fer
60th Regiment of Foot, First Battalion	Lower Canada: Boucherville, La Prairie, Longueuil (Headquarters). Upper Canada: Kingston
60th Regiment of Foot, Second Battalion	Lower Canada: Côteau du Lac, Lachine, Montreal
Royal Artillery	Lower Canada: Fort William Henry

Arriving on the Niagara Peninsula, Edward landed at the small settlement of Newark after having passed the formidable Fort Niagara. He had arrived at one of the very edges of the British Empire, and it must have seemed a veritable outpost in the young Royal's eyes. P. Campbell offers a wonderful description of the village as it would have appeared during the Prince's tour:

> Opposite the fort of Niagara, on a large flat point on the Canadian side of the river is a town laid out and lots given gratis to such as will undertake to build on it agreeably to a plan laid down by the government ... half an acre is allowed for the stance of each house and garden, and eight acres at a distance for enclosures, besides a large commonty reserved for the use of the town. Several people have taken lots here already and no doubt, as the community advances in population, so will the town in building.[33]

The Prince progressed up to Navy Hall and The Commons (an area of land behind Navy Hall owned by the Crown) to be greeted by the Simcoes and other assembled colonial dignitaries: Chief Justice William Osgoode, Attorney General John White, Secretary William Justice, Receiver General Peter Russell and his half-sister Elizabeth, a few officers and their ladies,[34] as well as a large delegation from the Six Nations of the Grand River assembled under the direction of Sir John Johnson to meet, in the words of Simcoe, the "Son of their Great Father."[35]

Originally built by British craftsmen from Fort Niagara, Navy Hall was the only building of note at the time of the Royal Tour, but was still under extensive renovation. Recognizing himself as far from the palace of Westminster, Simcoe described his future legislative assembly in a letter to British parliamentarian James Bland Burges:

> I am fitting up an old hovel, that will look exactly like a carrier's ale-house in England when properly decorated and ornamented; but as I please myself with the hopes that some future "Gentleman's Magazine" will obtain drawings of the first Government House, the first House of Assembly, Etc., and decorate it with the "Aude, Hospes, contemnere opes" [dare, guest, to despise riches] of old Evander ...[36]

Indeed, Government House (the office residence of the lieutenant governor) comprised three marquee tents on The Commons that the Simcoes had purchased from equipment left from Captain Cook's ill-fated third Pacific expedition of 1779. Elizabeth Simcoe commented that the tents commanded a beautiful view of the river, and because Navy Hall was not yet ready, the Prince would be given them for his stay. Meals would have been served in one of the marquee tents, but there are also stories that the Prince dined in the local pub, the Harmonious Coach House (famous as the building captured, occupied, and burned to the ground by American forces during the War of 1812 before being rebuilt as the Olde Angel Inn).

After arriving at Newark on August 20, the Prince went immediately to Fort Niagara across the river. The stone fort was still in British hands, although it occupied territory contested by the Americans, and the Prince's visit highlights the uneasy political situation along the frontier. The issue of control of the western forts (forts Niagara, Schlosser, Oswego, and Detroit) were a contentious one between the Americans and British. After the 1783 Treaty of Paris, these forts remained in the hands of the Crown, although the Americans were quick to point out that they were on United States soil. In the face of possible American aggression, Simcoe, himself constantly lobbying for the increased militarization of Upper Canada, issued a memorandum from Montreal on June 21, 1792 addressing the issue. Just before entering Upper Canada, Simcoe called for the demolition of forts Niagara, Oswego, and Detroit, and that the lands they inhabited be included within a new Indian Territory.[37] Simcoe's stance contradicted Lord Dorchester's 1787 letter from then-Home Secretary Viscount Sydney, stating that Britain's intention was to keep the western posts and that the governor would be expected to do whatever was necessary to ensure their safety.

Edward's visit to Fort Niagara reaffirmed Lord Dorchester's intention to retain the outposts. While at the fort, the Prince was given the customary royal salute, which included the firing of a cannon, much to the lieutenant governor's misfortune. Elizabeth Simcoe explained in her diary that "when a Salute was fired the Gov. was standing very near the Cannon & from that moment was seized with so violent a pain in his head that he was unable to see the Prince after that day …"[38] One month after Edward's departure, the lieutenant governor presumptuously informed George Hammond (British envoy to the United States) that his view remained that the forts on the American side of the Niagara River should be razed.[39]

Meeting with the assembled First Nations peoples, Edward watched a ceremonial war dance and was given the name "Chief-Above-All-Other-Chiefs." The Prince's presence along the frontier was seen as strengthening the alliance the British desperately needed to maintain with the First Nations in order to survive in the region. The visit of a son of the King demonstrated which side of the Northwestern War the British were on, and the Prince would later write to his father:

> A very large deputation from the Indians of all neighbouring nations came to Niagara to wait my arrival, as soon as they heard that I was to visit Upper Canada. Their professions of attachment to Your Majesty and the British Government were extremely warm, and they would not on any account return home to their tribes till they made me faithfully promise that in the name of them all I should inform you, in the strongest words I could find, of their zealous attachment to your person, and of their utmost readiness at all times to obey any commands with which you may at any time chuse [*sic*] to honour them.[40]

The Prince's use of the word "nations" in reference to the deputation is deliberate — referencing the wording of the Royal Proclamation of 1763, which addressed the "several Nations or Tribes of Indians" — reaffirming their equal relationship with the Crown.

After his meeting with the First Nations, the Prince travelled to Niagara Falls, stopping at the encampment of the Queen's Rangers (Simcoe ensured that his old regiment would be a fixture in the new province) at what would become Queenston Heights. Edward stopped for refreshments at the Georgian residence of Robert Hamilton (member of the legislative assembly) before moving on to forts Schlosser (also in American territory) and Erie.

So impressed was he by the Queen's Rangers that Edward asked for volunteers from the regiment to be transferred to his Royal Fusiliers. To the undoubted annoyance of the lieutenant governor, all men five feet nine inches and over were ordered to parade in front of the Prince on the 26th of August, but Simcoe was quick to remind them that any transfers were purely voluntary.[41]

The Prince visited Upper Canada in its infancy and his presence highlighted the very foundations of the society that Simcoe intended to nurture. Although the lieutenant governor's requests for more soldiers, a central capital, and universities would be ultimately frustrated by the British government, a unique "Loyalist" identity was partially seeded in the great peninsula. This idea would be greatly enhanced following the successful conclusion of the War of 1812 a few years later.

Near the end of his letter to the King summarizing the visit to the new province, Edward approached his father with a plan that would have put him right in the middle of the Northwestern War with America:

> May I presume now, Sir, to request your permission for me to visit the American States in the winter at the close of 1793 or commencement of 1794, in case it should be your Majesty's intention that I should be at that period in this part of the world. Two months, or ten weeks at the utmost, would enable me to visit any part which it is an object for me to see, either in a military point of view, or as a traveller, according to the best information which I have been able to obtain.[42]

It was the French Revolution that would change the course of Edward's time on the continent, although he would get his wish to become the first member of the Royal family to visit the United States of America.

5

Life in Lower Canada and War in the West Indies, 1792–1794

Returning from Upper Canada on September 13th, the Prince was addressed by the citizens of Montreal at Château Ramezay, Dorchester's Montreal residence. The assembled citizenry told Edward of Montreal's approval of the new 1791 Constitution while he stood outside the vice-regal residence. Three months later, at the opening of the newly proclaimed Lower Canadian Legislature in Quebec City on December 17, 1792, Prince Edward was again regaled with statements of loyalty from the appointed council and elected assembly. These were followed by similar announcements from the clergy and citizens of Quebec, Montreal, and Trois-Rivières, who referred to the Prince as "the son of the best of sovereigns." Edward responded by referring to the people as "the King's old and new subjects," "the French and English inhabitants," reiterating his assertion at Charlesbourg that they were all "the King's Canadian subjects."[1] However, it seems that some aspects of his trip to Upper

Canada had haunted Edward, since privately he was harbouring some serious concerns for the future of the provinces.

In a letter to William Dalrymple, groom of the bedchamber to the Duke of Clarence, Edward (despite what he said at the event) was having second thoughts about the viability of Canada two weeks before the first sitting of the Lower Canadian Legislature. The Prince even went as far as predicting the inevitability of Canada following the United States' path to Revolution:

> In a fortnight, the assembly of this country will meet; I fear on reflecting on the ignorance, the stupidity & the want of education of the major part of the members of the lower house, we may expect something not unlike a Polish diet.[2] Certain it is, that there is the most inveterate Jealousy subsisting between the French & English inhabitants, & the most sensible & experienced people here seem to fear that the new constitution was not perfectly well timed. The situation of France[3] having occasion'd such a general fermentation, I may say all over the world, it is certainly to be feared that the same spirit which has manifested itself even in England may sooner or later work on the minds of the people here, & be productive of consequences which can be paralleled only by those thro' which England unfortunately lost the American colonies: I sincerely wish that I may be a false prophet on this subject but I believe I may say that I am not singular in my fears.[4]

Edward kept his concerns over French-English unity away from the general public; instead he tried to enforce the idea that these two European cultures were now united under his father's Crown. Publicly, the Prince cultivated some wonderful interactions with the people of Lower Canada, including a popular story of dancing with a one-hundred-year-old woman from Île d'Orléans after she told him that her life wish was to dance with the son of the Sovereign.

In early 1792, the legendary Montreal theatre company *Les Jeunes Messieurs Canadiens*[5] (scorned by the Catholic clergy for their controversial plays) performed in Quebec under the patronage of Prince Edward and the Royal Fusiliers. During the opening of Quebec's first theatre hall that year, the Montreal company made the following announcement:

> This town owes its first performance hall to its enlightened benefactors. The immortal master-pieces of the French stage came before science, allowing it to develop.... Their march here will be the same ... but when they at last flourish, they will carry to our posterity the great name of Edward....[6]

A curious claim by the community of Sorel, then called "William Henry" (named after the Prince William during his brief visit to the region in 1787, but reverting back to its original name in 1845), has Prince Edward visiting the governor general's summer residence, or "Governor's Cottage," during his time in Canada. The local Anglican church, Christ Church, claims that Edward patronized their parish (the Royal Arms that hung over his pew remains) during his time as commander-in-chief of British North America, but since the Prince was not resident in the province at that time (1799–1800) this seems unlikely. It is more plausible that the Prince visited the community and its church during 1792–93 and stayed at the governor's cottage as a guest of Lord Dorchester.

On September 5, 1793, the Quebec Sunday Free School opened, with Prince Edward as its patron. Again he appears as a figure through whom the disparate European cultures of Canada could find common ground. The *Quebec Gazette* announced:

> From an ardent desire of promoting the happiness and prosperity of his [*sic*] Majesty's faithful subjects of this Province, and from the experience of the many and great advantages that have been received from the Sunday Schools in England ... His Royal Highness Prince Edward has been pleased strongly to recommend to the subscriber to open a Sunday Free School for the benefit of all those of every description who are desirous of acquiring the necessary and useful branches of education, and will conform to the rules and regulations that will be made for that purpose.[7]

Rule five is particularly interesting: "Reading, writing, and the various branches of arithmetic, shall be constantly taught in both languages; particular care taken to render the acquisition of the English language as easily as possible, to His Majesty's new Canadian subjects."[8]

A moment of excitement in the settlement was created on November 10, 1793, two days after a ball in honour of Prince

Edward's third birthday being celebrated on the continent, when a fire broke out on Rue Sault au Matelot in Quebec's lower town. Working alongside Lieutenant Governor Alured Clarke, Edward helped to put out the fire, much to the delight of the community. The Lower Canadian Legislature praised the Prince for "the ardent zeal and indefatigable ability which His Royal Highness displayed on all occasions, for the protection of their property and the security of their lives."[9]

It was around this time that Captain Frederick Augustus Wetherall of the 11th Regiment of Foot informed the Prince that a resident of Quebec had caught wind of a mutiny being planned by some of his soldiers. The uprising involved between ten and twelve members of the Royal Fusiliers, including Privates James Shaw, Joseph Draper, William La Rose, and Timothy Kennedy, and Sergeant Thomas Wigton, all of whom planned to capture and assassinate the Prince. When James Shaw confessed after being interrogated, he identified his associates. Dr. William Anderson wrote a dramatic account of the capture of William La Rose:

> The Prince, knowing the desperate courage of the man, and the danger that must be incurred in attempting his arrest, himself headed the party that went in pursuit, and surprised him while sitting at a table at Pointe aux Trembles [near Montreal]. "You are fortunate, My Lord," said La Rose, "in my not being armed, for By Heaven, if I had had my pistol I would have blown out your brains."[10]

Edward himself wrote to Sir William Fawcett (adjutant general to the British forces[11]), "I look upon La Rose the

Frenchman to be one of the deepest, most disgusting & most dangerous villains that it is possible to meet with."[12] Born on the Isle of Jersey in the Channel Islands, La Rose had joined the Royal Fusiliers in Gibraltar and had a reputation for being a hot-headed and rebellious trouble-maker.[13] It is important to note that La Rose was not French Canadian as some Quebec accounts have asserted.

A general court martial was convened and the men involved convicted — William La Rose spoke of their intention to march the regiment into the United States and present it as a gift to President George Washington (La Rose had served with him during the American Revolution). Joseph Draper was sentenced to death, William La Rose to three hundred lashes (although Dr. Anderson records that the sentence was the maximum allowed — 999 lashes), Timothy Kennedy to seven hundred lashes, and Thomas Wigton to four hundred lashes and a demotion to private. After being lashed, some accounts — most likely fictional — record William La Rose turning to face the Prince, and after striking his own forehead, saying, "It is the bullet, my Lord, and not the lash, which ought to punish a French soldier."[14]

Fearing that Edward's strictness would be circulated in England as the cause of the abortive mutiny, Sir Alured Clarke wrote to Sir William Fawcett himself to exonerate the Prince. The mutineers, Clarke asserted, were soldiers who Edward had transferred into his regiment at Gibraltar on account of their "size & good looks" (i.e. elegant extracts).

"These have unluckily prov'd to be men of bad morals & desperate characters," Clarke explained, "& amongst them, one in particular nam'd Rose, who is a native of France & has been in various services, which, it is probable, he has left with marks of infamy."[15] Worried that King George III would think that the Prince was in any way at fault for the actions of the mutineers in his regiment, Clarke continued, speaking specifically to concerns over Edward's strictness: "The Prince has lately made some prudent alterations that he thought might be proper & give satisfaction, which, I am told, is the case; & as everything seems to go on well at present, I trust & doubt not, but it will continue."[16]

The whole affair came to an end in April 1793 with the traditional death march by Joseph Draper, who, surrounded by his regiment, followed his coffin to an open grave. Kneeling on the ground to be shot, Draper was informed by the Prince that he had successfully lobbied the lieutenant governor for the mutineer's pardoning.[17] The Prince had also been able to secure the remittance of Timothy Kennedy's sentence, saying that the private was not very smart and would not have been a part of the mutiny if he had been sober at the time.

Despite all of this excitement, Prince Edward was painfully bored of Lower Canada. In his letters to his father, he tactfully hinted of a desire for a transfer back to Europe, but was much more direct when writing to the Prince of Wales. "I must own that though this country is preferable to Gibraltar, by the liberty one enjoys of ranging about," Edward wrote to his older brother before departing for his tour of Upper Canada, "I dread the next winter, as I am convinced that it will be still more stupid & insipid than the last."[18] Edward's letters home would increase in frequency throughout the following year as the French Revolution escalated into a continental war.

On January 21, 1793, King Louis XVI was executed to the horror of Europe's crowned heads. Two weeks later France's declaration of war against Great Britain caused a great mobilization of the upper classes. War with the French meant the opportunity for quick promotion and even glory for the British aristocracy — and the sons of King George III were eager to prove themselves. Like General Isaac Brock a few years later, Prince Edward was frustrated at being locked in Canada — thousands of miles from the European battlefields. Hearing of the new state of war between Great Britain and France, Edward immediately wrote to the King asking for a reassignment with his regiment to the European theatre of war: "I cannot help feeling the greatest anxiety when I reflect at what a distance I am at this moment from your person ..."[19] That same day Edward penned a letter to his brother, the Prince of Wales, asking him to use whatever influence he had to make a transfer possible. Edward added:

> In May next, as you must recollect, I shall have been eight years absent from home, and if after so long an absence, five years of which I have been serving in the line of my profession, when I request to be permitted to return home, solely for the purpose of being more useful to my country than I could be by remaining in Canada, I am to meet with a denial, I cannot help thinking that such usage would be most cruel, and hard indeed.[20]

After hearing that the Prince of Wales had approached the King on his behalf, Edward wrote to thank his brother one month later, re-emphasizing his determination to serve in Europe. By August of the same year, Edward was getting desperate — and his tone to the Prince of Wales had noticeably changed:

I shall not trespass on your time with any relation of the cruelty of my situation in being left in
this dismal country in a state of utter inactivity,
when, from my profession I should be on actual
service, ... I mean that while they are employed
on the brilliant field on the Continent I am left
to vegetate in this most dreary and gloomy spot
on the face of the earth, where there is not the
most distant chance of there being anything
like service.[21]

The Prince of Wales was lobbying on his brother's behalf
for a transfer to Europe. Henry Dundas, now also the secretary of state for war (appointed in 1794), responded to a letter
from the Prince of Wales informing him that Prince Edward
had already written on the subject! Agreeing with both Princes,
Dundas recommended Edward to Lord Amherst, commander-
in-chief of the British forces in Europe, suggesting that he serve
in either the West Indies or Southern France. Amherst, in turn,
presented Prince Edward's original letter to the King, who then
agreed that his son should be sent to the West Indies as a major.
general under the command of the venerable Sir Charles Grey.[22]

Edward was elated. Upon hearing of his promotion and
reassignment, the Prince wrote to his father in the opening days
of 1794:

Permit me to offer to your [sic] Majesty the
assurance of my warmest gratitude for the high
honour you have conferred upon me in pro-
moting me to the rank of Major-General [again
outranking Simcoe!], and more particularly for

the very great favor which you have conde-
scended to shew [*sic*] me by appointing me to
the Staff of the Army in the West Indies under
Sir Charles Grey.[23]

Edward does not forget to add at the end of his letter:
"Before I conclude ... [I will] express a wish that when the active
service of the campaign in the West Indies ceases, your [*sic*]
Majesty will have the goodness to think of posting me to some
other station of activity ..."[24] For the time being the King did
not have another station in mind, and Lord Amherst informed
the Prince that once the war was over in the Caribbean he
would be expected to return to Canada.

It being January, and since the interior of Canada harboured no ice-free ports at that time, Prince Edward would
have to cross into the United States to make his way to Boston
to meet a ship destined for the West Indies. Julie de St. Laurent
left Quebec for Halifax, where she would catch a ship bound for
New York before heading to England on May 10, 1794, to wait
out Edward's service. Before leaving for the frozen territory of
the United States, Prince Edward and Madame St. Laurent bid
adieu to their friends in Quebec — particularly the de Salaberry
family. Farewell gatherings were held throughout the settlement,
including one hosted by the Freemasons.

Prince Edward had been appointed provincial grand master
of Lower Canada in 1792 by the Antients' faction of the Masonic
order (he had entered the fraternity in 1789 while in Geneva).
This was not unusual, since most of the world's English-speaking
elite — whether it be Joseph Brant, George Washington, John
Graves Simcoe, Thomas Jefferson, or Sir John Johnson — were
Freemasons. So ubiquitous was the organization that south of

the Canadian border a significant number of the American founding fathers of the United States were members of "the Craft," while a few decades later Upper Canada's first Parliament likely met at Newark's Freemason's Hall.

From 1751 to 1813 the Freemasons had been divided into two camps — called the Antients (Ancients) and the Moderns. The Antients believed that the Moderns had moved away from the teachings of Freemasonry, and advocated a return to the traditional practices and rituals. Edward was initiated into the fraternity as a Modern (the Prince of Wales, and later Prince Regent, was head of the Moderns from 1792–1812) but was rumoured to lean more toward the Antients form of Freemasonry. When Edward was appointed as provincial grand master in Quebec by the Antients' Grand Lodge (he was installed June 22, 1792), he brought both camps together in Lower Canada and provided another link between the province and its new mother country across the Atlantic. John H. Graham's 1892 *Outlines of the History of Freemasonry in the Province of Quebec* credited the Quebec masons for creating the union that British masons had so longed for.[25] Such sentiments emphasize the link Freemasonry had with British imperial identity. In her 2007 book, *Builders of Empire: Freemasons and British Imperialism*, Jessica Harland-Jacobs writes, "Prince Edward … embodied the link between Freemasonry, loyalism and empire building that was then developing and that would become a hallmark of the Craft in the nineteenth century."[26]

The masons hoped that the unity created by Prince Edward's appointment would continue beyond his time in Quebec, and they bade farewell to him as he prepared to leave for Boston in 1792, saying, "We have a confidence and a hope that under the conciliatory influence of your [*sic*] Royal Highness the Fraternity in General of Freemasons in His Majesty's dominions will be united." To this the Prince replied, "You may trust that my utmost efforts shall be exerted that the much-wished-for union of the whole Fraternity of Freemasons may be effected."[27] Edward would stay true to his word, and remained provincial grand master of Lower Canada until 1810.

Later, on December 1, 1813, the Prince, who was now back in England, succeeded the Duke of Athol as grand master (leader) of the Antients. Three weeks later, on December 27th, Edward proclaimed the Articles of Union between his Antients and the Moderns, now headed by his brother Prince Augustus Frederick, the Duke of Sussex. Before proclaiming the union, both royal brothers initiated the other into their respective expressions of the order. Afterward, Edward walked the Duke of Sussex to the Masonic throne, proclaiming him the grand master of a united brotherhood under the United Grand Lodge of England.[28]

Leaving Quebec on January 22, 1794, Prince Edward found himself about to enter the republic of the United States of America, a country still trying to settle into a constitution and government that did not include King George III. A political chasm had opened up around the future of the federal government between the anti-federalists (a group that believed in strong state governments), represented by Thomas Jefferson, and the federalists (a group that believed in a strong national government supported by the elites of society), headed by Alexander Hamilton.

New York City, a microcosm of the new country (and federal capital from 1788–90), had been left in ruins after the last British transport left in 1783. The Loyalists had left a settlement of 12,000 souls on "Evacuation Day" that, by 1794, had grown to around 35,000, including roughly 1,000 slaves — slave ownership had started growing again in the city by 1790.[29] The city was also awash with political refugees from the French Revolution — they even had their own French-language newspaper (the *French and American Gazette,* renamed *Gazette Français* in 1796). English traveller William Strickland is quoted as saying in 1794 that "the City is so full of French that they appear to constitute a considerable part of the population."[30] Still dressing in the old bourbon-style, the émigrés paraded around the city in their full powdered wigs, golden-headed canes, silver-set buckles, and cocked hats. Possibly because of the social developments identified above, King George III did not want his son in New York, the largest city in the United States. A frustrated Edward wrote to his brother the Prince of Wales:

> I am under the necessity of going by way of Boston, every other route, but through the United States being absolutely impracticable, at this advanced season of the year; it would have shortened the distance of my journey very considerably, had I gone by way of New York, but Lord Amherst, having signified to Lord Dorchester, His Majesty's disapprobation of my going that way, that of course precludes my taking that route. The very moment that the roads are passable I shall set off, which I imagine will be about the 19th or 20th, in which case, if, as I expect, I am fortunate enough to [be] meeting the Hussar frigate at Boston, I may reckon at being in Barbados, in five weeks from the present time …[31]

Prince Edward crossed into the American republic by way of Lake Champlain, becoming the first member of the Royal family to do so since the rebellion.[32] Unfortunately for Edward, the ice

The political divisions of the United States of America during Prince Edward's 1794 visit.

was not thick enough to support the weight of his luggage, and the sleds carrying his "baggage, consisting of what plate, linen, clothes &c. He then possessed"[33] crashed through to the bottom of the lake. Financially, this was a devastating loss to the Prince. Forever in debt, the Prince knew this accident ensured that whatever gains had been made by his father in assuming the costs incurred in Gibraltar were wiped out.

Edward's first point of formal entry into the country was at Burlington, Vermont. Having entered the United States in 1791, Vermont had become the fourteenth state, not yet three years before the Prince's arrival. Prior to that, Vermont had operated as a virtually sovereign state (issuing its own stamps and coinage) despite being claimed by New York State since 1783. Many in Britain agreed with John Graves Simcoe in believing that the state could still be swayed to return to the imperial fold.

No writings from the Prince himself about his visit to the United States survive; although a few interesting scraps have surfaced to shed some light on American interactions with a member of their former Royal family. William Anderson found letters from the Prince's time in Burlington that seem to support the idea that there were those in the state who still expressed a degree of deference toward the Crown. The first was written to the Prince by local residents Elnathan Keyes (a justice of the peace before the Revolution), John Bishop, and William Prentice, requesting an appointment where Edward could receive "that respectful attention tied to your rank, and you may be assured, although in a strange country, that protection is equally at your command, with the greatest subject of the United States."[34] Edward granted the men an audience.

A wonderfully imaginative anecdote written by a resident of Vermont in 1794 is more of an insight into the rejection of the Crown as part of the new culture of the United States:

Prince Edward ... being in the northern part of the state of Vermont, on a tour from Canada to Boston, happened, it is said, to call in at a House of a worthy citizen, who followed the occupation of a taylor. The prince with his attendants and his miss, feeling in high spirit, and observing the woman of the house to be a decent good-looking person, and probably forgetting [sic] for the moment his recent transition from his father's regal domain, to the Columbian Republic, he caught the woman in his arms, and forcibly obtained a kiss, asking her husband at the same time how it made him feel to have his wife kissed by a prince. The husband more keenly netled [sic] by the insult than the indecency of his [sic] Royal Highness, plied his foot nimbly and repeatedly to his posteriors, asking him in turn, how it made a Prince feel to have his breech kicked by a Taylor.[35]

Arriving in Boston on February 6 to receptions that ranged from awe to unrestrained contempt, Edward discovered that no ship waited in the harbour to whisk him away to the West Indies and he would have to wait for the dilapidated small six-gun packet (mail ship) *Roebuck*[36] to arrive from Halifax.

Boston was at the heart of the lore surrounding the American Revolution; home of the infamous "massacre" and subsequent tea party, Paul Revere, and the Battle of Lexington and Concord that started the war. The idea of a son of King George III entering the city seems ill-advised. Yet, not only did Prince Edward enter the city, his arrival was celebrated by many of its citizens.

Local author Samuel Adams Drake wrote about Edward in 1899, not as the son of a great tyrant, but rather as a respected visitor to his city:

> In December, 1794, the Duke of Kent, or Prince Edward as he was styled, was in Boston, and was received during his sojourn with marked attention ... The prince was accompanied to Boston by his suite. He was very devoted to the ladies, especially so to Mrs. Thomas Russell (prominent Boston merchant), whom he attended to the Assembly at Concert Hall. He danced four country-dances with his fair companion, but she fainted before finishing, and he danced with no one else, at which every one of the other eight ladies present was much enraged. At the British Consul's, where the prince held a levee, he was introduced to the widow of a British officer ... It was well said by one who knew the circumstance, that had his Highness settled a pension on the young widow and her children ... The prince visited Andrew Craigie [key figure during the American Revolution and then a very wealthy developer and Alexander Hamilton insider]. He drove a handsome pair of bays with clipped ears, then an unusual sight in the vicinity of Old Boston.[37]

Edward stayed with the British consul Thomas McDonogh and used the extra time to attend a wedding, as well as a dance held at the Boston Concert Hall. Edward also attempted to attend a performance at the newly opened Federal Street Theatre, also called the "Boston Theatre."

Three days after the Prince's arrival in Boston, the Federal Street Theatre had been opened by British-born actor and theatre manager Charles Stuart Powell, with a performance of Henry Brooke's *Gustavus Vasa*. Almost immediately a debate raged around the theatre being opened with the playing of the French revolutionary anthem "*Ça Ira*" (some theatre-goers demanded the playing of this song as well as "Yankee Doodle"). The Prince found himself placed in the middle of this controversy, as recounted in a letter written by Bostonian Sarah Flucker to her friend Lucy Knox:

> On Monday I went to the Play, but alas no Prince — he was prevented by the assurance that a large Party was formed in the Gallaries to Govern Music and Preside for the Night — and very properly put himself out of the way of Personal insult — which the Mob Prove doubtless ripe for — for whatever the Box door opened, and he was supposed to enter, there was an alarming opposition between the ragamuffins, Loyalists & Orchestra and Peace could only be obtained by mortifying submission of the good to the bad. All *Gentlemen* [Federalists] were *silent* — the Jarvis Clan [Anti-Federalists] gave words of command....[38]

The orchestra's refusal to play French republican songs highlighted very real divisions in Bostonian society in 1794, a decision that would eventually erupt into violence (glass and other debris was thrown from the gallery into the orchestra pit). For many Americans, the French revolutionaries were going too far as they purged their country of its aristocracy. For others, the French Revolution (imbued with its "Declaration of the Rights of Man and of the Citizen") was naturally tied to the ideals of the American Republic. According to Flucker's letter, it was the Anti-Federalists who commanded the respect of the mob — meaning it was a good thing that Edward stayed away from the theatre that night.

Plagued by financial problems (a problem Edward would have sympathized with) theatre manager Charles Powell would eventually be invited by Prince Edward to resettle in Halifax in an effort to elevate the arts in that community. Powell arrived in Nova Scotia in 1797.

Even though he enjoyed himself as he moved within Boston's high society, Edward's eye must have always been on the Boston piers, hoping for the arrival of the leaky *Roebuck*. The window of opportunity for a young officer to be promoted through battle currently being provided by the French Revolutionary Wars could be closed at any moment, and Edward must have grown impatient with each passing day. However, nearly a month would elapse before Prince Edward departed Boston for the West Indies on March 15, leaving the British Consul McDonogh to report to London:

> [I]t is much to be regretted that it was not conve-
> nient for his [*sic*] Royal Highness to make a lon-
> ger stay as his Engaging manners and conduct
> would tend very much to dissipate the Prejudices,
> with which many in this Country are strongly
> tinctured against Royalty and princely Blood,

and would also unquestionably strengthen the British interest in America.[39]

Edward's presence in the United States highlighted the strong feelings — and divisions — that the Crown evoked in American society. It had only been eleven years since the conclusion of the Treaty of Paris, and many Americans (including those who drafted the constitution) still did not know which direction their political institutions should take. The Prince became a focus, attracting public curiosity, adulation, and protest (the first two being reactions commonplace today when Americans come into contact with the Royal family). Simcoe was right in suggesting that there were still strong monarchist leanings in the United States, and Edward's brief tour of the country brought many of those feelings to the forefront. Had any of his future tours to America (one would be planned for 1801) taken place, the influence Edward may have had on the relationship between the United States, Britain, and, eventually, Canada may have been significant.

For now, Edward's interests were elsewhere as he eagerly looked south to the West Indies. Reporting to his father of his arrival on the island of Martinico (present-day Martinique) on April 4, 1794, Edward proudly wrote that he was stationed outside of the French Fort Bourbon and had already taken fire during one of the many engagements of the French Revolutionary War in the Caribbean.[40]

Having long been the quiet plantations of Europe, controlled by different masters an ocean away, the West Indies found themselves as one of the theatres of a global war initiated by an erratic French Republic.[41] The Haitian Revolution (1791–1804) and the French abolition of slavery in 1794 (reinstated by Napoleon in

1802), signalled the beginning of radical change for the traditional, slave-based economies. As well, British and French forces were hopscotching across the region, tearing down each other's flags along the way.

Such an environment was exactly what Prince Edward needed — the constant state of war and conquest afforded many opportunities for a young man to prove himself in battle. He was desperate to make a name for himself, particularly to redeem his reputation in the eyes of his father. Infinitely proud of the improvements he had made while in command of the Royal Fusiliers (better discipline, cleaner appearance, less drunkenness), Edward also wanted to show he could be effective in battle. He had his chance during the brief Battle of Martinique.

Under the command of Admiral Sir John Jervis and General Sir Charles Grey, an expedition had landed on Martinique and successfully took control of the island's principal settlement of St. Pierre. With both Forts Royal and Bourbon remaining to be conquered, Edward joined these campaigns upon his arrival from Boston on April 4, 1794. Just twenty days after having set foot on the beach of Martinique, the Prince proudly wrote to his father:

> Permit me to take the earliest opportunity of congratulating your Majesty on the entire submission of the Island of Matinico to your arms. I look upon myself as peculiarly fortunate in having been able to reach this before the trenches opened on Fort George (late Fort Bourbon), principal fortress of this country, having thus been able to follow the progress of the siege from the very commencement of the first battery ... I was fortunate enough to

be named by the Commander-In-Chief to take possession on the 23rd, at the head of the Grenadiers, which brigade I am posted to, of the gates of the fortress, and I am at this moment returned from attending the ceremony of the French Garrison laying down their arms, and their embarkation in consequence.[42]

The need for affirmation from the King drips from each line as the Prince relished his opportunity to report on the events (and his participation in them) in Martinique. Edward also participated in the swift capture of the islands of St. Lucia and Guadeloupe (gripped in the chaos created by the abolition of slavery) before the end of the month.[43] With the campaign ended for the summer (and the beginning of hurricane season) Edward drafted another letter for the King from Guadeloupe with a few interesting, and very forward, suggestions.

Acknowledging that once everything was over he would be expected to return to Canada, Edward wrote, "I shall proceed immediately on my return to Canada, but propose first putting into Halifax, and there remaining till the arrival of the May Packet [mail], in the hopes of being honoured with your [sic] Majesty's orders relative to the application which I took the liberty of making to you through the Commander-In-Chief, for the removal of myself and my regiment to Nova Scotia ..."[44] The Prince was determined not to be sent back to Quebec, hoping instead to be posted to the port of Halifax — a community that allowed for speedier access to the American coastline, the West Indies, and England.

Edward continued his letter with another hopeful anticipation of the King's wishes: "I think it my duty at the same time to mention that if another campaign is commenced in the Autumn in the West Indies under the command of Sir Charles Grey ... I intend [on] ... rejoining him in this part of the world."[45] The Prince went on to say that his father's silence on the matter would be interpreted as agreement with Edward's plan. The lack of any alternative orders, by Edward's logic, meant that the Prince was perfectly meeting the King's wishes by returning to the West Indies the following autumn.

Concerning his hope of not being posted in Quebec, Edward's presumptuous plan to base himself in Halifax was exactly what both King George III and Lord Amherst had in mind. Concerning the other two requests, the Prince would prove to be disappointed. Rather than be spirited home thanks to his triumphs in the Caribbean, Prince Edward was appointed commander-in-chief of the King's forces in Nova Scotia and New Brunswick. Edward's time in Halifax would last nearly six years, transforming the community into the most fortified British outpost on the North American coastline, as well as injecting new life into what had originally been a garrison town filled with Loyalist refugees. For Halifax it was the dawn of a golden age, for Edward it was one of the most important roles he would ever fill.

6

Prince Edward's Golden Age of Halifax, 1794–1800

Little did Edward know as HMS *Blanche* sailed into Halifax Harbour on May 10, 1794 (hours after Julie de St. Laurent had departed for England) that this settlement would be his home for the next six years. In his book on Halifax, Nova Scotian historian Thomas Raddall wrote that before the Prince's arrival in Halifax the settlement had been "a struggling, shabby wooden town defended by the tumbledown remains of forts hastily thrown up or repaired at the time of the American Revolution."[1] When the Prince departed the provincial capital as the Duke of Kent in 1800, Raddall boasted that Edward left a city with "excellent public and military buildings and surrounded by powerful batteries ... with a new and lofty tone to its society and a vigorous outlook on the world. For a century afterwards the Haligonians talked of Edward's time as a golden age."[2]

It is true that the Halifax that greeted its new resident was a shadow of what it would become before Edward left. Founded by

Colonel Edward Cornwallis (uncle of the famous Lord Cornwallis of the American Revolutionary War) and a motley group of colonists in 1749, Halifax was named for George Montagu-Dunk, Earl of Halifax, the president of the British Board of Trade and Plantations, who had come up with the idea to settle the region. A garrison town, Cornwallis' Halifax was filled with brothels, pubs, idle soldiers, and sailors, all centred around a wooden fortress perched atop its crowning Citadel Hill.

Nicknamed "Nova-Scarcity" for its lack of everything (housing, supplies, even hope) by Loyalists during the American Revolution, the province (and Halifax in particular) was becoming an

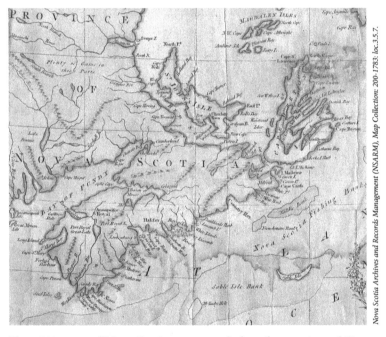

Nova Scotia Archives and Records Management (NSARM), Map Collection: 200-1783: loc.3.5.7.

The 1783 map of Nova Scotia, one year before the creation of New Brunswick (cartographer unknown), labels Prince Edward Island as St. John's Isle. Residents petitioned the island government for the new name in 1798.

important base of operations for the British. Nova Scotia's population on the eve of the American Revolution had been 20,000, half of which were from New England. An influx of approximately 15,000 Loyalists flooded into the province following the 1783 Treaty of Paris, joining the Mi'kmaq, Acadians, Northern Irish, Scottish, and Germans already there.[3]

In fact, the sheer amount of new settlers to the province necessitated the creation of New Brunswick in 1784, thus allowing for more government jobs for the displaced elites from America. Colonel Thomas Carleton, Lord Dorchester's younger brother, became its first lieutenant governor.

Another of the "elite" refugees to land on Nova Scotia's docks was John Wentworth, former British governor of New Hampshire, and his wife, Frances. After fleeing New Hampshire in 1778, the Wentworths sailed to England. In 1783, the former governor returned to North America as surveyor general, basing himself

Office of the Lieutenant Governor of Nova Scotia.

Sir John and Lady Wentworth's portraits attributed to John Singleton Copley (1738–1815) hang in Government House, Halifax. Notice Lady Wentworth's pet rat.

in Nova Scotia. The ensuing years saw the couple make the necessary social connections (and, as written earlier, in these efforts Frances was quite accomplished) to assure John Wentworth's appointment as lieutenant governor in 1792.

It was as lieutenant governor of Nova Scotia[4] that John Wentworth boarded the HMS *Blanche* to welcome Prince Edward to Halifax, triggering days of celebrations in the settlement. Wentworth quickly became the father figure that Edward so desperately wanted. A week later, Wentworth supported the Prince in a letter to his friend John King, the undersecretary of state in London:

> [Prince Edward] informs me of his writing home, from the West Indies, to obtain the command of this District, in which he is extremely interested and earnest to succeed and has also displaced the *Earl of Moira* [a government vessel] to Lord Dorchester, soliciting this arrangement, and to have his own Reg. Sent here ... I most sincerely wish He may succeed to this command. It would delight the whole province ...[5]

The Prince had a renewed confidence in himself since his successful service in the West Indies, and now wanted to expand his responsibilities in the continent. If he became the commander-in-chief of the Nova Scotia and New Brunswick forces, Prince Edward would have considerable influence in the military development of the Maritimes. John Wentworth supported Edward's request, penning a letter to Henry Dundas (which would be passed on and read by the King) advocating the same.

Whether or not he saw potential in the Prince as a strong military commander is uncertain, but John Wentworth was an ambitious man, who likely coveted the prospect of having a son of the King so close at hand. Still, Wentworth seemed to be genuinely impressed with the demeanour of Edward. "The Prince is adored here," Wentworth continued, "a perfect confidence is entertained here of his military knowledge. His deportment is correct, dignified [sic] and irresistibly conciliating [sic]."[6] He shrewdly commented that if Edward was given military command of the region he would send for Madame de St. Laurent immediately, writing "I am persuaded her Society will be extremely useful."[7]

While Edward waited for news from England, he busied himself by touring both Nova Scotia and New Brunswick over three weeks, departing Halifax on June 14. According to the records, he tackled the difficult roads on foot, bound for Annapolis Royal, likely stopping en route in Herring Cove and St. Margaret's Bay before boarding HMS *Zebra* at Digby for Fredericton, where he inspected a detachment of the King's New Brunswick Regiment and met Lieutenant Governor Carleton on the 21st of June. Carleton, who had plans to make New Brunswick the military centre of the Atlantic colonies, was quickly frustrated upon hearing of Edward's plans to have his headquarters at Halifax. Leaving the interior of the province, the Prince travelled to Saint John and Fort Howe to inspect its batteries and ordinance on the 23rd of June.

This was not simply another Royal tour, but rather a survey of what could potentially become Edward's jurisdiction if his request from the King was granted. Returning to Annapolis Royal, Edward stayed at the house of Colonel James DeLancy at Round Hill (where an unlikely legend persists that a lonely Prince kissed a serving maid behind a door during a reception[8]), and danced the night away at a ball held in his honour at Loyalist Joseph Totten's house. Attended by another Loyalist, Captain James Moody of the Royal Nova Scotia Regiment,[9] who was beloved by the Loyalist settlers as one of the most effective British raiders during the American Revolution,[10] Edward likely travelled to the Sissiboo River (near present-day Weymouth) visiting the Acadian settlements of the area before returning to be feted by the people of Digby. Once back in Halifax, Edward continued his correspondence with his friend Louis de Salaberry. His first letter, dated July 14, 1794, concerned de Salaberry's eldest son, Charles-Michel.

Prince Edward had supported Charles-Michel de Salaberry, helping the boy join the army when he was fourteen. Now that the lad was sixteen, Edward delivered on a promise to his friend and gave Charles-Michel a commission in the West Indies. Unfortunately, Louis's son left for the Caribbean just as Edward was returning north. Calling Charles-Michel his "young protégé," Edward pledged to watch over the boy's career, a promise he would keep for the rest of his life. In a separate letter to Louis's wife, Françoise-Catherine, Edward offered his assurance that Charles-Michel would be transferred back to Canada as soon as the opportunity presented itself.[11]

Apart from the future of Charles-Michel, the Prince's letter to Louis de Salaberry also touched on an event hanging over the Catholic Church of Quebec:

> I have learnt with sincere regret the loss you have sustained in the Coadjutor,[12] the more so as I am confident your present Bishop is in no way qualified at the present time to fill the place he occupies. I very much fear that the office will

be filled long before my letter will reach the
hands of Lord Dorchester, as it recommended
your good friend M. Renauld, for whom I entertain the most sincere esteem, and also reminded
my Lord that you had been most strongly recommended to him by me, at the moment of my
departure, and that I hoped he would not lose
sight of the promise he then made me, to be
useful to you.[13]

This passage is written by a much more confident Prince
Edward, who was now trying to directly influence Canadian
affairs (and those of the Catholic Church). The former coadju-
tor to the bishop of Quebec had been the pro-British Charles-
François Bailly de Messein, the same man who had baptized
Edouard-Alphonse de Salaberry (Prince Edward's godson).
De Messein had been sent to Paris for his university education in 1755, returning to Quebec after the British Conquest.
Ordained in 1762, the young priest would preach loyalty to the
British Crown during the American Revolution and afterwards
become tutor to the children of Lord Dorchester, even travelling
with them during trips to England. When Jean-François Hubert
became bishop of Quebec in 1788, it was Dorchester who
appointed de Messein as his coadjutor and heir, even though
the two men did not like each other.

Ultimately, it was a proposal for a mixed-denominational
university (which would have appealed to Prince Edward since
his Quebec Sunday School was opened to all religions) to be
created in Quebec that split the two bishops down the middle —
Hubert was opposed to the idea while de Messein was supportive
to the point of publicly denouncing his superior. By April 1790 all

communication between the two bishops had broken down, and de Messein had become *persona non grata* in Quebec. That it was de Messein who had baptized Edouard-Alphonse de Salaberry back in Quebec gives credit to the belief by the Roman Catholic Church that the sacrament was not sanctioned; meaning Prince Edward and Julie de St. Laurent were not the boy's legitimate godparents. Bishop Charles-François Bailly de Messein died on May 20, 1794, after finally making peace with Bishop Hubert.

By nominating the unknown Maskinonge parish priest, M. Renauld (his first name has been lost) as coadjutor, Prince Edward was trying to influence the selection of the heir to the powerful diocese of Quebec and head of the Catholic Church in Canada. Ultimately, Renauld would be rejected by Hubert, who appointed Pierre Denaut (he had a firm allegiance to Rome) coadjutor and heir on June 29, 1795. Hubert had told Dorchester of his plans to appoint Denaut six days after the death of de Messein, but until Denaut's formal appointment, Edward would continue to advocate for Renaud.

Once back in Halifax, apart from a series of tours, levees, and other social events, Edward could only wait for word from England concerning his purpose in Nova Scotia. A double blessing presented itself in August 1794 with the arrival of the *Westmoreland* from England, carrying not only Edward's new orders, but also Julie de St. Laurent. The King had consented to Edward's request to be appointed commander-in-chief of His Majesty's forces in Nova Scotia and New Brunswick, and also agreed to the Prince's moving his headquarters to Halifax. This appointment was the first real display of trust in the Prince freely given by his father, and Edward relished the appointment. By staying in Halifax, Edward was also assured of the continued generosity of the Wentworths.

Nova Scotia Archives, 201104004.

The Lodge, the country retreat owned by the Wentworths, 1817–18, as depicted in an oil painting by John Elliott Woolford (1778–1866). Although Edward and Julie had not visited The Lodge for nearly twenty years when this painting was begun, Woolford imagined what the estate must have looked like during Halifax's "Golden Age."

Nova Scotia Archives, 201104005.

Ruins of The Lodge as painted by Irishman William Eager (1796–1839) in 1838.

Undoubtedly the vice-regal couple were overjoyed at the prospect of hosting Edward and Julie for the near future, and they immediately set out to make the couple as comfortable as possible. The Wentworths kept a small residence outside of Halifax called Friar Laurence's Cell, a reference to the previous owner, John Lawrence, and the Wentworths' love of Shakespeare (it was Friar Laurence who, among other things, agreed to marry the tragic lovers in *Romeo and Juliet*). Once Julie de St. Laurent arrived in town, the Wentworths immediately offered apartments at Government House to the couple, as well as providing their country retreat with its two-hundred-acre view over the Bedford Basin. Renovated and expanded, the estate was rechristened "the Lodge" and soon became the social hub of the province. Today, Haligonians refer to Edward and Julie's home outside of the city as "Prince's Lodge."

In a 1971 article, Mollie Gillen quotes Nova Scotia historian G.E. Fenety's description of the Lodge after he visited the site in 1828. Even though it had been abandoned for nearly twenty years by the time Fenety entered its gates, a sense of the region's "golden age" still remained among the ruins:

> The ruins of the dining room walls were papered with old-fashioned landscape scenes, representing the English chase, in which deer, foxes, horses and riders, green fields, hedgerows, trees, streams, and high barred gates, formed the picture.... The Lodge stood one-hundred and fifty feet from the road — in front of which grew Lombardy poplars, tall and conical, over topping all the other trees of the forest; and skirting the road to the full

width of the property was a paling fence with the scattered remains of what was once a well kept hawthorn hedge.... The grounds about and in rear of the dwelling gave evidence of having in their prime been well cared for. The formation of the beds in the garden was still visible. The walks through the umbrageous forest were in a good state of preservation ... winding through those sequestered and deserted avenues — one running into another — away back into the dense forest. I suppose there must have been over a mile of these walks, if placed in continuation. There was an artificial lake a few hundred yards in the rear of the dwelling — on one side of which was a wooden Chinese temple, which afforded a cover and shelter to the sportsman, who might throw his line out of the door or window ... upon a hot summer day.... Then there were other ornamental houses and grottoes scattered around the grounds here and there, inviting leisure and repose to the wanderer in search of the picturesque, especially when the hospitalities of the place brought together large numbers of the gentry and their ladies from town.[14]

The gardens of the estate were lush, filled with peach, nectarine, apricot, and plum trees, as well as raspberry bushes, honeysuckles, tulips, roses, carnations, violets, crocuses, lilies, and six blue Peruvian Squills.[15] Sprinkled around the property were ponds, including one rumoured to be cut in the shape of a heart. Sixty years after the departure of Edward and Julie, the grounds were visited by his grandson, Prince Edward (the future King Edward VII). In preparation for the 1860 visit to the region a new, smaller pond was created in the shape of a heart where the original had once been. During his visit to the area, the Prince of Wales collected some sweetbriar from the grounds of the estate and sent them back to his mother as a souvenir of her father's time in the province.[16] The 1860 heart-shaped pond remains as the centrepiece of Hemlock Ravine Park, which now occupies the former site of the Lodge, part of the Rockingham community in the Halifax Regional Municipality.

The other remnant of the Lodge is its small rotunda built on a mound along the shoreline looking back towards Halifax Harbour. Built for the Royal Fusiliers' regimental orchestra, the

Photo by Mike Milloy

The heart-shaped pond as it appears today in Hemlock Ravine Park, the former site of the Lodge. This pond was created for the 1860 royal tour of Prince Albert Edward, Prince of Wales (the future King Edward VII).

single-roomed building was perfectly positioned to fill Bedford Basin and its surrounding hills with music. Lined with thin columns (disproportionate to the size of the building), the rotunda is crowned with a large golden ball. Frescos and paintings created by Edward once adorned the interior walls.

Low-lying barracks were constructed along the nearby shoreline of Bedford Basin to house two companies of the Royal Fusiliers. The site also included a series of signal towers that used combinations of flags and torches to stay in touch with Fort George on Citadel Hill. After Edward's departure in 1800, these barracks became the Rockingham Inn, which was a summer retreat for Halifax's wealthy classes as well as home to the elite "Rockingham Club."[17] This fraternity was an exclusive group known for enjoying the inn's music, refreshments (ginger beer was a favourite), and amazing views over the bay. The club met regularly until disbanding a few years after the Wentworths left the province in 1808.[18] The Rockingham Inn survived until it burned down in 1833.

In 1794, with the British Empire still in a state of war with France, Prince Edward's interests in the region extended far

Photo by Nathan Tidridge.

Prince Edward's rotunda as it appears today along Bedford Basin near Halifax.

beyond the establishment of his residence. Fearing that Halifax was under direct threat of a French invasion (there were reports that New England timber was being harvested to build French warships), Edward ordered royal engineer Captain James Straton to draw up plans to transform the settlement into British North America's premier military complex.

Six months after having arrived in Nova Scotia on November 11, 1794, the Prince included Straton's sketches (with financial estimates) in an extensive report to Henry Dundas. Among other things, the report included a £9,339 plan to rebuild Halifax's citadel Fort George (named after King George II in 1749) "to contain 1,000 men with log bomb-proofs for 650 men, a magazine for powder to contain 1,200 barrels, and one for provisions to contain all kinds of species for three months."[19]

Work on Fort George and its surrounding battlements atop Citadel Hill, which began immediately, included shaving fifteen feet of earth from its top. As well as building himself a house on the north flank of the hill, Edward gave offices and a workshop to the Royal Engineers next to the northern barracks, and ordered that the fort's southern barracks be greatly expanded. More earthworks were added around the fort, as well as new offices, storehouses, and guard houses in downtown Halifax. In the centre of the settlement, the Grand Parade (a military parade square from the founding of Halifax in 1749) was shaved down to become level with Barrington Street and surrounded by a stone wall and iron railing.

The renovation of Halifax's Fort George involved many craftsman and labourers drawn from across the province, which, in turn, led to a labour shortage. By then many Nova Scotians had already left the province to seek better-paying work in the New England states, and experienced craftsmen were hard to find. Edward was desperate for men to fill his construction quotas. His prayers were answered when over 550 Maroons (guerrilla warriors descended from African slaves of Jamaica who had been exiled to the province at the conclusion of the island's last Maroon War, 1795–96)[20] sailed into the Nova Scotia harbour. When the Maroons arrived in Halifax on July 21 and 22, 1796, Edward travelled to the ships by launch to welcome his fellow exiles. Impressed by their new linen uniforms and "height, bearing and physique of the [Maroon] warriors ... [and] their strength and vigour,"[21] and seeing their potential as a source of labourers for his ambitious construction program, Edward wrote to William Henry Cavendish-Bentinck, Duke of Portland, who had succeeded Henry Dundas as home secretary in London:

> The Maroons were landed a few days after their
> arrival and disposed of in as comfortable a man-
> ner as could be done at the very short notice we
> had of their arrival, since which, at their own
> free will, and option, a part of them have been
> daily employed in the new works on the Citadel
> Hill, at the same pay as His Majesty's troops.[22]

As well as providing equal pay for the Maroons working on Fort George (memorialized by the "Maroon Bastion," which was destroyed during the construction of the current incarnation of Fort George that was completed in 1856), Edward also ensured they had provisions, lodging, and clothing.[23] Some of the Maroons were also employed as paid servants at Edward and Julie's Lodge.

Edward's vision went beyond the settlement of Halifax to the construction of five Martello towers, named after a virtually impregnable fort on Cape Mortella, in Corsica, to be built along the Nova Scotian coastline. Named after Edward's older brother, the Prince of Wales Tower and its surrounding fortifications were also designed by Captain Straton. Work on the original tower began in 1796 without approved funding from the British Board of Ordinance, which, not surprisingly, provoked a stern reprimand from officials in London.[24]

Both Prince Edward and John Wentworth (now "Sir John" after being awarded a baronetcy in 1795) were present at the ceremony for the laying of the cornerstone for the Prince of Wales Tower. Able to accommodate two hundred men, a Martello tower was a new development in coastal defences. An extremely expensive venture, the Prince of Wales Tower was constructed of local stone with a wooden snow roof (distinguishing it from its European counterparts). With walls eight feet thick at their base, and a super structure that reached twenty-eight feet into the sky, the tower dominated its location on Halifax's Point Pleasant, guarding the approach to Citadel Hill. Finally completed in 1797, the imposing tower (despite being in need of constant repair) would eventually be joined by the Duke of York Tower (1798), Duke of Clarence Tower (1798), Fort Charlotte Tower (1812), and Sherbrooke Tower (started in 1814, but not completed until 1828).[25]

Turning his attention to Halifax Harbour, Edward ordered the refortification of George's Island (named after King George II), replacing its old works with a star-shaped fort, named Fort Charlotte after Edward's mother. A battery (York Redoubt), constructed at the entrance to Halifax Harbour, was linked to Fort George and Sambro Island at the Atlantic entrance to the Bedford Basin, using Edward's telegraph system based on signal flags, black balls of wicker, drums, and lanterns. Within the harbour, a crescent-shaped battery of cannon was added to the existing Fort Ogilvie, and Fort Sackville was built (including the addition of a new barrack) on the mouth of the Sackville River in the Chebucto Basin. In case any ships slipped past these defences, Edward ordered a chain boom (a string of logs connected by iron chains that spanned the width of the harbour) laid across the basin — the ring that attached the boom to Point Pleasant, called "Chain Rock," still survives.

Edward's telegraph system was expanded to connect Halifax to Windsor, forty miles away, and finally to Annapolis Royal, (for a total distance of nearly 124 miles) where the Prince laid the cornerstone of the new officer's quarters at Fort Anne. Considered revolutionary for its time, North America's first "telegraph" system allowed for the dissemination of information across Nova Scotia in record time. By 1798 it had been extended into New Brunswick, running as far north as Fredericton. With all of this in mind, it should not be surprising to learn that during Edward's time in Halifax he was spending £100,000 a year on fortification projects.

Edward also remained keenly interested in his Royal Fusiliers and Wentworth's Royal Nova Scotia Regiment, and, as he had done with Simcoe, the Prince transferred some of the best of the lieutenant governor's regiment to his own. The Prince's correspondences from this period are filled with requests to England for proper pouch belts, bayonet belts, and gun slings for the Royal Nova Scotians — Edward even recommended a £50 per year pension for the widow of one of the officers. Numerous letters exist in which the Prince pleads for funding to properly garrison the region with hundreds of soldiers, but there was no money to be had. Throughout his time in the Maritimes, Edward toured the provinces, inspecting his soldiers personally whenever he could.

On February 29, 1796, the British and Americans rati-
fied Jay's Treaty, named after John Jay, the chief negotiator for
the Americans. Designed by Alexander Hamilton, the treaty
settled many longstanding disputes between the two countries
following the Treaty of Paris, including trade agreements, the
need for compensation to the American government for dam-
ages incurred during the Revolutionary War, and the continued
British occupation of the western forts bordering Upper Canada.

That March, Lord Dorchester received his orders to vacate
the western forts, and when that was accomplished, the governor
general indicated that he was ready to retire home to England.
Throughout the final years of his time in British North America,
Dorchester had become disillusioned by the decentralization of
power that was occurring, as evidenced by John Graves Simcoe's
habit of going over Dorchester's head and dialoguing directly
with officials in London. On February 20, a frustrated Lord
Dorchester wrote to the Duke of Portland: "[Y]our Grace will
perceive that this command, Civil and Military, is greatly disor-
ganized" and "everyone is impatient of Restraint."[24] Letters from
the previous five years between Dorchester and Simcoe speak
to not only their mutual dislike, but also the power struggle
between the offices of governor general and lieutenant governor.

Anticipating Dorchester's intention to retire, Prince Edward
began lobbying for his own appointment as commander-in-
chief of all British North America. It was Edward's belief that
Dorchester's high position would be broken into two: a military
commander-in-chief and civil governor general. Writing to his
brother the Prince of Wales on January 20, 1795, Edward (newly
promoted to the rank of lieutenant-general) reasoned that he
alone had the experience needed to be commander-in-chief.
Asking the Prince of Wales to advocate on his behalf to the King,

Edward wrote, "[W]ith this feather in my cap, which is the first in my profession in this part of the world, I shall be more cheerfully to bear with a continuation of my banishment."[26]

It became clear that Sir John Wentworth's efforts at cultivating a friendship were paying off as Edward put forward his candidate for the civil office of governor general:

> I am the more particular in making my present application as I have been informed that it has long been intended that the posts of Commander-in-Chief and of Civil Governor-General should be separated; for if I conceived that it were still intended that the same person should hold both, I never should think of applying for the situation, as the work would be far too arduous for my abilities ... I know it would be the height of the ambition of Governor Wentworth to be named to the post of Governor-General should the separation of the two situations take place; indeed a more zealous, deserving, and useful servant his [*sic*] Majesty does not possess. His appointment would be particularly agreeable to me, as I am convinced from our mutual knowledge of each other, since I have been in the command here, that we should perfectly harmonize together, by which the public service would be much benefited.[27]

Hearing of the government's intention to send Lieutenant-General Robert Prescott to North America as commander-in-chief, a despondent Edward wrote to Major-General Edmonston

(British general during the American Revolutionary War) on December 27, 1795, "I am to endure this mortification of seeing an officer sent out over me to succeed to the supreme Command/General Prescott named to this station."[28] A career soldier in the British Army, Robert Prescott had spent many years fighting for the Crown. Prescott served as aide-de-camp to Jeffery Amherst during the Seven Years' War, attained the rank of major-general during the American Revolutionary War, and served with Prince Edward at Martinique and Guadeloupe during the French Revolutionary Wars. Returning to England in 1795 due to poor health, Prescott now found himself crossing the Atlantic again.

As the spring of 1796 warmed over the Maritimes, Edward still held out hope that the King only intended Prescott for the civil half of Dorchester's office. Writing to Louis de Salaberry in a letter dated March 13, 1796, he remained confident that it was his destiny to become commander-in-chief.[29] Edward recommended de Salaberry's son Charles-Michel (who, after serving with distinction in the West Indies, had just arrived in Halifax that summer) to the staff of the incoming governor on July 2, also promising Louis de Salaberry that he would endeavour to have his friend nominated as an executive and legislative councillor, "the *first*, for the hundred pounds which belongs to it, and the *second* for the honor of the thing."[30] Eight days later everything changed.

On July 10, 1796, it was proclaimed in Quebec that General Prescott would take command as both lieutenant governor of Lower Canada and commander-in-chief over all the provinces. Prince Edward was devastated. Writing to his friend General William Edmeston (Loyalist hero of the French and Indian Wars) an exasperated Edward vented:

General Prescott arrived in Canada on the 19th
of June, & on the 9th of the following month,
succeeded Lord Dorchester in British North
America with the local rank of General. I imagine that the hopes I had entertained of having
a separate command from the General over
Nova Scotia & New Brunswick were totally
without foundation, for not a Single Syllable of
anything to that purpose has transpired, & on
the contrary, by the General orders given out at
Quebec, it appears decided that everything is to
go on as in His Lordship's time …"[31]

Edward tried to remain positive, writing, "In the mean
while, I am not losing my time, for I always endeavour to keep
both myself and every one about well employed,"[32] but the effect
of Prescott's appointments must have been crushing. It is perhaps this moment more than any other that firmed the Prince's
resolve to be sent back home. Becoming governor general would
have been a display of confidence in Edward by not only his
country, but also his King and (more importantly) father.

"The highest friend I have has been much dejected …" wrote
John Wentworth to John King in the spring of 1797. Wentworth
goes on to quote Prince Edward as saying, "I am now near thirty,
and the only one of the Brothers, kept abroad, and now the only
situation fit for me is govern [is given to someone else] over my
head, while I am on the spot. It is so pointed against me that I
cannot stay in the Country with any satisfaction, or regard to my
own Honour."[33]

His desire to be commander-in-chief of all British North
America (even after the appointment of Prescott) can be seen

in a fearsome defence of its authority against what Edward saw as ambitious subordinates. During the summer of 1797, Prince Edward had sent recruiters to the various settlements, themselves dangerously short on soldiers, in order to fill his quotas needed to garrison Halifax's defences. Lieutenant Burton of the Royal Fusiliers was dispatched to Newfoundland, and his arrival in St. John's prompted a stern letter to Edward from the island's governor, Admiral William Waldegrave: "I now find myself under the very disagreeable necessity of being compelled to inform your Royal Highness that you seem to be wholly unacquainted with the nature and powers of the Commission I have at present the honour to hold from His Majesty."[34]

Claiming astonishment at Edward's attempt to take soldiers from his island, the governor reminded the Prince that he held a commission as "Governor and Commander in Chief in and over our Island of Newfoundland in America, and the Islands adjacent, including the Islands of St. Pierre and Miquelon; and also of all our Forts and Garrisons [the governor underlined these words] erected and established, or which shall be erected & established in our said Island."[35] To Governor Waldegrave, Lieutenant Burton's presence in Newfoundland was an affront to the authority of the King's representative and Prince Edward needed to be put in his place.

Newfoundland had become the first colony of the British Empire when it was claimed for the crown of Queen Elizabeth I by Sir Humphrey Gilbert on August 5, 1583. Since the arrival of Gilbert, a unique system of governance had developed for the island, beginning with the practice of "fishing admirals." During the sixteenth and seventeenth centuries the island's principal harbours fell under the seasonal control of the masters of the first ships to enter them. This system survived until 1728 when

Captain Henry Osborne of the Royal Navy was appointed naval governor over the island.

Naval governors, or "floating governors," were admirals of the Royal Navy, who exercised authority over the entire island (including the "fishing admirals") during their time in the colony (usually from June-July to October or November) as well as commanding the naval squadron at St. John's. The job was a unique balancing act between the needs of the fishing admirals, the Royal Navy, and the residents of Newfoundland. For an admiral, the rules aboard a ship (i.e. the captain's word is law) served as a template in governing the colony and administering law — a perspective that Prince Edward would not tolerate.

Waldegrave's idea of the scope of the King's representative of Newfoundland was similar to John Graves Simcoe's interpretation of the same office in Upper Canada. On the issue of who was supreme in British North America, Edward held the opinion shared by Lord Dorchester that the governor general was the highest representative of the King on the continent, whereas Simcoe and Waldegrave held that the governors were the highest authorities in their individual provinces.

On August 26, 1797, Edward responded to Governor Waldegrave's lecture with a lengthy essay on the authority of the governor general as commander-in-chief.

"When I received His Majesty's orders to take upon myself the Command of the district of Nova Scotia and its dependencies," Edward began:

> I was ordered to address myself to Lord Dorchester [Edward would also cite Robert Prescott's commission as governor general, which had the same wording], then holding

His Majesty's Commission of General and
Commander in Chief of His Majesty's Forces
in the Provinces of Upper and lower Canada,
Nova Scotia, including the Islands of St. John
and Cape Breton, New Brunswick, and within
[underlined by the Prince] the Island of
Newfoundland in America."[36]

Edward asserted that as commander-in-chief of all British
North America, Lord Dorchester had been the supreme commander "without exception." Including letters and memoran-
dums from as far back as 1788, the Prince supported his argument
that concerning military matters in the provinces and colonies of
British North America, the governors and lieutenant governors
were subordinate to the governor general (presumably this argument extended to civil government as well). "I cannot acknowledge any superior but him," Edward underscored to Waldegrave.

Edward also pointed out that Governor Waldegrave, as an
admiral in the Royal Navy, did not have any jurisdiction over
land forces stationed in Newfoundland. Using Waldegrave's own
words against him, the Prince asserted:

I therefore hope that as on your part you are
pleased to say "that you trust I shall on due con-
sideration think too favourably of you to suppose that you could ever sacrifice your duty, your
honour, and your understanding to the mere
opinion of an Individual, however great may
be his personal merits, or elevated his situation,
whilst your own reason and long Precedent con-
vince you that you ought not to do so," You will

in like manner have the candour to believe, that
nothing but the highest sense of Military honour, and the fullest conviction of doing my duty
correctly as the Officer to whom [Governor]
General Prescott's authority in this district is
delegated, can induce me to be as firm in my
opinion as to the point of discipline now under
discussion, as you are in yours.[37]

Edward goes even further in the letter, informing Waldegrave
that he had committed a great error in asserting his supremacy
in Newfoundland, and that it was important that the admiral
understood that he personally was subject to the control and
orders of the commander-in-chief of British North America.
That Prince Edward held a commission issued by the governor
general and commander-in-chief meant that the governor of
Newfoundland, in many areas, was also subject to orders issued
from Halifax (in Prescott's name). After educating Waldegrave
about the chain of command in British North America, Edward
concluded to the governor that Lieutenant Burton of the Royal
Fusiliers was in Newfoundland to visit the senior officer of the
land forces stationed at St. John's (Colonel Skinner), not the
naval governor. The Prince finished his letter by saying, "I conceive Your Excellency will probably judge it proper to report
these matters home,"[38] assuring the governor that he would do
the same (sending copies to both the governor general and the
King). Edward would get his soldiers from Newfoundland.

Edward's letter to Waldegrave was a passionate defence of the
power of the governor general as commander-in-chief of British
North America. The Prince's reasoning reflects the views of Lord
Dorchester that Canada needed a strong central government

under which the various provinces and districts were subject. As a source of authority, the Crown evoked by Prince Edward was the same envisioned by the Fathers of Confederation sixty years later.

Still, for the time being Edward was not to be supreme commander-in-chief and not even a letter from King George III, commending his son for his good work on the continent, could shake the desire to return home. Expressing joy at receiving a letter from his father, Edward replied on April 23, 1798: "It has long been the height of my ambition to learn from yourself that my conduct since you have been pleased to employ me actively in your several foreign possessions has met with your approbation ..."[39]

Initially agreeing with the King that his time in British North America likely spared the Prince from continuing the bad behaviour that had begun in Geneva, the letter dramatically changed its tone after acknowledging the King's promise of a return home after the end of the war with France. Begging his father not to make him spend another winter in Halifax, Edward enclosed two letters from local officials stating that, for health reasons, the Prince could not endure the cold weather another season. A similar appeal was sent to the Prince of Wales.

Aware of Edward's feelings, Sir John Wentworth addressed the Prince on behalf of the Council and Assembly of Nova Scotia on July 7, 1798, in a show of appreciation for his work in Nova Scotia:

> Your Royal Highness's Military Talents and eminent abilities invariably directed to the support of good order and the Honor of His Majesty's Crown and Government have secured to us

the advantages of peace in the midst of a War which has desolated a large proportion of the rest of the World.... The many essential services which Your Royal Highness has rendered to this Province will long be remembered with gratitude by us and cannot fail to interest His Majesty's subjects most sincerely in your future Glory and Happiness.... In the hope that Your Royal Highness would be induced to receive from the Province some mark of its gratitude and affection, the Legislature has unanimously appointed a Committee[40] with instructions to provide and present to You, in the name of the Province, a Star, which we humbly request you will be pleased to accept as a Testimony of the attachment we have to Your Royal Highness ...[41]

The "star" the Nova Scotia Legislature promised to present Edward with was a diamond-encrusted emblem of the Order of the Garter (the Prince was made a knight of the Order by the King in 1786). Such a gesture would not have been lost on the Prince, who, as always, found himself financially distraught. Forever conscious of looking his part as a Prince, the replacement for Edward's wardrobe lost under the ice of Lake Champlain in 1794 had been captured by French forces the following year. The French navy captured two more wardrobes in 1795 and 1796, costing the Prince over £8,000.00 to have them replaced.

Thanking Wentworth, the Council, and Assembly, Edward replied that he had always intended to perform his duties in such a way that honoured the King. "To have succeeded therefore," he continued, "in this object of which circumstance your address today affords me so honourable a testimony, is the more gratifying to my feelings as I flatter myself when his Majesty is informed of it, he will not hear it with indifference."[42] Poignantly, Edward made no mention of wanting to continue his role as commander-in-chief over Nova Scotia and New Brunswick, nor to stay on the continent. Sadly, the Royal Archives and Royal Collection report that the whereabouts of Edward's diamond star remains unknown, perhaps sold to pay off some of his debtors.

A blessing in disguise occurred on August 8, 1798, as Edward cantered through the streets of Halifax. Catching its hoof in a wooden drain, the Prince's horse fell and rolled over him twice, crushing Edward's left thigh against some rocks. When days of rest and medical attention did not alleviate the bruising and pain, Edward had the excuse he needed to request an immediate transfer to England.

Asking Prescott for formal permission, Edward sent for Dr. Nooth in Quebec to produce a certificate prescribing the waters of Bath in Somerset, England. News of the Prince's accident, and its assumed consequence, travelled across the continent to Upper Canada, where William Osgoode wrote to Peter Russell that the *Earl of Moira* had arrived in Quebec with orders commanding Dr. Nooth's attendance to a contusion on Edward's thigh (John Wentworth would comment that the doctor made the fastest journey between Quebec and Halifax on record). Osgoode reported: "the prevailing Suspicion is that his R.H. wishes for the Doctor's Sanction upon the Necessity of his going to Europe.… This harmless Stratagem is certainly allowable considering his Honourable Banishment during the prime of his Life."[43]

With Nooth's agreement forwarded to King George, Edward and Julie de St. Laurent boarded HMS *Topaze*, arriving at Spithead in Hampshire on November 14. A letter from his brother the Prince of Wales awaited Edward, instructing him to head right for Windsor and the open arms of his family. It was a far cry from his last homecoming. Church bells rang out across the country and people sang out in welcome as the Prince made a dash for Windsor Castle.

Unbeknownst to him as he made his way to his family, back in British North America, Edward's greatest honour had been passed by Governor Edmund Fanning of the Island of St. John. Frustrated with being confused with the settlements of Saint John (New Brunswick) and St. John's (Newfoundland), the legislature in Charlottetown voted to change the island's name to Prince Edward Island on November 29, 1798.[44] The island had fallen under the jurisdiction of Edward as commander-in-chief over Nova Scotia and New Brunswick, and he had ordered the construction of new barracks and harbour fortifications for Charlottetown. The island's new name was accepted by King George III on February 2, 1799, coming into effect on June 3, 1799. Since then Prince Edward Island has been the greatest monument to Edward's presence on the continent.

In England, Edward was fully embraced by his family — his brother the Prince of Wales even held a grand dinner in his honour. Apartments were prepared at Kensington Palace (he moved in at the end of December), and while it is doubtful that Julie de St. Laurent was presented to the King and Queen, or Edward's sisters, she certainly mingled with the royal brothers during private gatherings. Formal balls and galas, attended by the entire Royal family, now filled Edward's time as Christmas and New Years provided more opportunities for celebration and time together. Later on in the summer, Edward even found himself counselling a reunion between the Prince of Wales and his long-time mistress, socialite Maria Fitzherbert.

Early in the new year, Lady Frances Wentworth arrived in England in time to witness a delegation from Nova Scotia (headed by her son Charles-Mary) present Edward with the diamond star promised earlier in Halifax. That spring, Edward was created His Royal Highness, the Duke of Kent and Strathearn, and Earl of Dublin, with an annual income of £12,000 established by the British Parliament. It had truly been a triumphant homecoming.

A few months later, in April 1799, Governor General Robert Prescott was recalled to London over the deterioration of his relationship with his executive council. Prescott had accused members of his council of deliberately trying to take lands for themselves that were already being developed by settlers. Edward had commented on the ineffectiveness of Prescott in a letter to Louis de Salaberry before leaving Nova Scotia for England, but was not aware of the rift that had developed between the governor general and his executive at the time.[45] With such a dysfunctional relationship between the governor general and his council, the British government feared their interests were in danger and ordered Prescott's return to London. Although the disgraced governor general would retain his position, Sir Robert Shore Milnes was sent to Lower Canada as lieutenant governor to run the colonial government.

Not keen on returning to British North America's climate (Edward had originally wanted to be commander-in-chief of India, but Henry Dundas vetoed the idea), the newly minted Duke of Kent was ever conscious of his financial problems (his new income would not make a dent in his debts as long as he stayed in London). With a heavy heart, Edward applied for the now-vacant post of commander-in-chief of British North America and was appointed to the position on May 10, 1799.

On July 25 Edward and his ever-present Madame de St. Laurent boarded the frigate *Arethusa* for the voyage back to

Halifax, arriving there on September 6. The Duke was not happy to be back, and from the beginning, he made it very clear that his time back in Nova Scotia was only temporary. Edward reiterated this in a letter to Henry Dundas (now British war secretary) penned two weeks after his arrival in Halifax: "I only came to this Country from a motive of honor and justice towards my Creditors, and certainly made a very good sacrifice in so doing ..."[46]

The Duke reminded the war secretary of their conversations, as well as those with the prime minister — William Pitt the Younger — and the King himself, about the possibility of Edward serving in Ireland. At the time, Great Britain was moving toward political union with Ireland (this came into force on January 1, 1801) and the Duke of Kent thought himself the perfect candidate for commander-in-chief there, or even in Scotland.

To his friend Louis de Salaberry, Edward was more upbeat, saying that his new appointment would afford him greater influence in matters relating to Canada, giving him the opportunity to provide de Salaberry with a good position within the government. This promise was fulfilled when Edward made Louis the Indian superintendent for Lower Canada upon the Duke's return to Nova Scotia.

Despite his trepidation at being back in North America, and his hope to be removed from the continent at the first opportunity, the Duke of Kent jumped into his work as commander-in-chief as soon as his boots hit the shore. One of his first actions was to begin the process of reorganizing the provincial regiments (which were restricted to their own jurisdictions and seldom crossed into another province's territory) so that they could serve anywhere in British North America. Ranks in the army would be recognized throughout British North America, rather than only the regiment's home province. Edward's idea of creating a "Canadian Corps" speaks to his use of the Crown to unify a disparate group of colonies through their loyalty to the King — it was the birth of the idea for a truly "Canadian" army.

Plans were also drawn up for an extension of Edward's remarkable telegraph system overland into Lower Canada and Quebec City. Earlier, when he and Julie de St. Laurent had arrived back in Halifax, news of their return had taken only forty-eight hours to travel as far as Fredericton over the telegraph network — a distance that would have taken a letter three to four weeks to traverse. Seeing the extension of the telegraph as a necessity in the face of American aggression to the south, as well as fitting into his plan to create a unified Canadian Corps, the Duke was unfazed by the staggering funds estimated for the project. In the end, the system was abandoned beyond the boundaries of Halifax and Saint John after the Duke's final departure from the continent. The system was briefly revived during the War of 1812 when American privateers threatened the Maritime coastlands, but again fell into disuse after 1815.

Halifax's construction boom continued despite the Duke's relieving Captain Straton of his duties over the construction of barracks for the Royal Military Artificers without Edward's expressed approval. With the appointment of Captain William Fenwick as commander of the engineering department, work resumed in the settlement — including the construction of some significant civic buildings.

Edward purchased Navy Island, an island across Bedford Basin from his Lodge, for the construction of a hospital to treat infectious diseases, as well as sponsoring many other projects, including the construction of St. George's Round Church (the Duke had a great respect for its congregation, who were descendants of German Protestants brought to Nova Scotia by Governor

Cornwallis to augment the English settlers already there[47]), and Halifax's famous Garrison Clock. As is seen with St. George's Church and the Rotunda at the Lodge, the Garrison Clock highlighted Edward's predisposition to round Palladian constructions, which were known for their symmetry, perspective, and values of the formal classical temple architecture of the ancient Greeks and Romans.

The Duke had ordered the clock from the Royal Clockmakers, the Vulliamy family of Switzerland, during his brief time in England. Designed by Captain Fenwick, the 1,000-pound clock was not completed until February 1801 (interestingly, the final payment for the clock was not received until April 17, 1802). Although the clock was originally intended to adorn a decorative

Halifax's famous Garrison Clock. The Duke of Kent ordered the clock to be built by the Vulliamy family of Switzerland in 1800, but it would not be installed in Halifax for another two years.

Photo by Christopher McCreery.

turret of the northern barracks of Fort George, many disagree-
ments over its final location raged during the years of its construction. Ultimately, a site was chosen on the eastern flank of
Citadel Hill at the head of George Street, where it can be found
today. The beautiful building Fenwick designed to house the
enormous clock was finally completed on October 20, 1803.

As in Quebec, the Masonic order had a long tradition in
Halifax, stretching back to the foundation of the settlement in
1749, with most of the prominent men of the province members
of various lodges. When Edward first arrived in Halifax in 1794,
he had been welcomed by the provincial grand master, Richard
Bulkeley. Edward was quite active in the region as a Freemason,
visiting Nova Scotia and New Brunswick's various lodges as well
as establishing new ones. Remaining the provincial grand master of Lower Canada, the Prince granted a charter to a lodge
in Detroit, then still claimed by the British. During his second
residence in Nova Scotia, Bulkeley asked Edward to lay the cornerstone for the settlement's Freemason Hall on June 5, 1800.
To commemorate the event, the Duke presented a silver bowl
to the province's first lodge, St. Andrews, founded by Governor
Cornwallis in 1750. The bowl remains in their possession today.

The Duke's most significant visitors during his eleven months
in Nova Scotia arrived in the fall of 1799 when the twenty-six-
year-old Louis Philippe, Duc d'Orléans, and his brothers, the
Duc de Montpensier and the Count of Beaujolais, unexpectedly
showed up on his doorstep. In exile from revolutionary France,
the brothers had left the Bahamas and arrived in Halifax aboard
the HMS *Porcupine*. During the previous four years, the royal
brothers had travelled throughout the United States and they
were now trying to get back to Europe, having heard of a possible restoration of the French monarchy following the "Coup

of 18 Fructidor" (the attempted seizure of power by pro-royalist forces in 1797).

The Duke had become a touch point on the continent for displaced French royals, directing them to safe communities across British North America. Still, he was shocked to find one of the claimants to the French throne in Nova Scotia. Edward related his surprise at finding Louis Philippe at his home in a letter to the Duke of Portland, dated November 21, 1799:

> Their arrival in the *Porcupine* Frigate from the Bahamas was one of the most unexpected, and I will candidly add, most disagreeable circumstances that could have occurred; they came in to the harbour very late in the evening, and the next morning at eleven they were at the door of a house in the Country ... where I am at present residing.... It was of course impossible for me to do otherwise than receive them with the politeness due to their birth; two days afterwards I met them at the Governor's, at dinner on his public day, and again after that, in the same place, on my own birthday. It therefore seemed unavoidable to invite them to dine at my house ...[48]

Originally supporting the Revolution, the Duc d'Orléans had fled France in 1793 as the government grew more radical. Edward knew of Louis Philippe's initial support of the revolutionary government, but no longer found any evidence of the Duc d'Orléans supporting republicanism or "democratic principles." Indeed, Edward had written an earlier letter to the Duke of Portland on behalf of the French exiles asking for safe passage to England (from where they intended to go on to Spain to visit their exiled mother), but he assured his superiors in London in his second letter that he only did so out of civility and hoped that his offer had not displeased the King. With no ships departing for England from Halifax, Louis Philippe soon left for New York. However, the Duc d'Orléans never forgot "the kind and generous attention" shown during his visit to the Prince's Lodge and later wrote in his autobiography that while in Nova Scotia he received an invitation by the Duke of Kent to reside in England (this detail was left out of any letters sent by Edward to the Duke of Portland).[49] A friendship would develop between the two men (as fellow exiles, they had much in common), with Louis Philippe frequently socializing and corresponding with Edward after his return to England. Louis Philippe would eventually be crowned King of the French on August 9, 1830, and the esteem he had held for the Duke of Kent was extended to his daughter, Queen Victoria, during her visits to France in 1843 and 1845.

During the winter months of 1799–1800 in Nova Scotia, the Duke prepared to take part in a series of extensive tours being planned for Cape Breton Island, New Brunswick, Prince Edward Island, Newfoundland, as well as Upper and Lower Canada. As commander-in-chief, Edward wanted to personally inspect the regions he was charged with protecting. However, despite these ambitious plans for the spring and summer of 1800, the bitter cold was too much for him. Putting an end to his plans for British North America, the Duke of Kent wrote to his brother Prince Frederick, Duke of York (as commander-in-chief of all British Forces), requesting a transfer at the end of May for reasons of health.

A considerable rift had opened between the royal brothers, and Prince Frederick, the Duke of York, had a habit of ignoring Edward's letters. The breaking point of the relationship may have been a letter sent by the Duke of York in the spring of 1800 responding to Edward's requests to be transferred to a command in either Ireland or Scotland. Bluntly denying his brother's request, the Duke of York lectured Edward about his mistress during their brief time in England:

> I am the last person in the world to preach or to wish to meddle in your private happiness or connections, but at the same time I must fairly say to you, you can have no idea how much the world talked of the public manner in which you went everywhere accompanied by Madame St. Laurent. I am perfectly well aware that this may be done abroad, but you may depend upon it that it cannot be done at home, and therefore I advise you as a friend to consider this subject well over.[50]

Despite whatever bitterness he held for the Duke of York, Edward was desperate not to weather another winter in Nova Scotia. On April 8, a dog spooked the Duke's horse as he rode along the King's Road in Halifax, causing him to be thrown off. Edward was dragged some distance after his leg became entangled in his stirrup. Nursing two broken ribs and a contusion on his face, Edward set out to respond to the Duke of York's letter.[51]

Avoiding direct confrontation over his brother's previous remarks, the Duke of Kent promised that if he was appointed to Ireland or Scotland he would maintain an acceptable distance from his mistress (separate homes isolated from one another). If Frederick was implying that Edward needed to end his relationship with Julie de St. Laurent to return to England, the Duke of Kent had strong words: "[If] I am to understand it is the intention to make my separation from Madame de St. Laurent a term without which I am not to be employed on the other side of the Atlantic, however, it is repugnant to my feelings to credit, I must at once declare that it is one which I will not admit to be dictated to me ..." With all of this said, Edward went on to write that if he was not permitted to return home before the next winter he had no choice by to resign his commission as commander-in-chief.[52]

At the same time as he wrote the Duke of York, Edward also sent a letter to the King, requesting his immediate return home, explaining that he was suffering severely from the effects of a blood disorder and that his chest was "so uncommonly weak that I am sensible nothing but your [*sic*] Majesty's permission to leave this country before the approach of the cold weather can secure me from the certain prospect of a severe attack ..."[53]

On June 17, 1800, the Duke of Kent got his wish when he received a letter from his father granting him leave to come home. Boarding HMS *Assistance* on a rainy August 4th, the Duke of Kent and Madame St. Laurent disappeared below decks as the residents of Halifax bade them farewell forever.

As Sir John Wentworth wrote to John King in England two days after the Duke's departure, "[The Duke of Kent] declares vehemently that he will never return to this Country again, even if he is obliged to retire from any active command ..."[54]

7

After Canada and Nova Scotia, 1800–1820

Back in England, the Duke of Kent and Madame de St. Laurent settled into their apartments at Kensington Palace and began fixing up an estate purchased at Ealing (West London) called Castle Hill Lodge. Now thirty-two years old, Edward had spent only eight months with his family since turning seventeen.

Although happy to finally be out of British North America, the Duke of Kent still maintained his prolific correspondences with the many officials and friends he met during a near-decade spent on the continent. Letters continued to pour in from people seeking patronage and advice on a whole range of topics related to the provinces. Two months after arriving in London, the Duke received a voluminous letter from John Graves Simcoe, asking for his support in obtaining the position of governor general of British North America.

Simcoe was aware that Edward still held the position of commander-in-chief (he would until 1802), and suggested that the two of them could work together to expand the former lieutenant governor's vision for Upper Canada to include the entire continent. Determined for the appointment, Simcoe even goes so far as to boast "I saved this country [meaning Upper Canada] from an American War … not only as the first gentleman, but as the first constitutional gentleman of the British Dominions."[1] Writing back, the Duke confided (undoubtedly to Simcoe's delight) that the separate offices of governor general and commander-in-chief would be perfectly combined in John Graves Simcoe. Edward also admitted that his main reason for retaining his command in Canada was financial, and hopefully would soon be replaced with a posting to Ireland or Scotland. Edward replied, "I am not desirous, unless it be in actual service, to cross the Atlantic again."[2]

While returning to North America was out of the question, Edward did not rule out a foreign posting all together. In fact, the Duke of Kent was eager to resume some form of service to the King, and pay off some of the crushing debt that still plagued him. With all of this in mind, on August 21, 1801, the Duke left the Royal Fusiliers to become colonel of the 1st Regiment of Foot ("the Royals"), who, many thought, was about to be posted to the European theatre.

Originally formed in Scotland by King Charles I in 1633 for service in France, the Royal Regiment was the oldest regiment in the British Army and had seen action in North America during the Seven Years' War (this included service during the 1758 Siege of Louisbourg). Steeped in legend, the 1st Regiment of Foot claimed its origins from the bodyguards of the ancient kings of Scotland. Upon the Duke of Kent's appointment as colonel, the regiment began to be known as simply "the Royals."

The French Republic was now undergoing its transformation into a European empire under the command of Napoleon

Bonaparte, who had himself declared "First Consul" December 12, 1799 (Edward and his brothers referred to him as "the Monster"). Even when the Treaty of Amiens was signed on March 25, 1802, declaring peace between France and the coalition formed against it (which included Great Britain), political and military leaders across Europe knew that it would only be temporary. Five days before the treaty was signed, the Prince of Wales wrote to the Duke of York informing his brother of Edward's determination to move his new regiment to the Mediterranean and become governor of Gibraltar. The Duke of York agreed, and on April 27, Edward and the ever-present Julie returned to the Rock.[3] It is at this point that Edward's military association with British North America formally ended; he surrendered his command at Halifax to become governor and commander-in-chief of His Majesty's forces at Gibraltar. The Duke arrived back at the Rock in an effort to return order to an outpost suffering from the lack of discipline. Edward's orders from the Duke of York, as his commander-in-chief, were quiet clear on the matter: "I consider it my duty on your assuming the command of the garrison at Gibraltar, to make your Royal Highness aware that much exertion will be necessary to establish a due degree of discipline AMONG THE TROOPS; and which, I trust, you will be able gradually to accomplish by a moderate exercise of the power invested in you."[4] The King was also rumoured to have implored Edward to try and curb the spending that had become the hallmark of his time in Halifax.[5]

On May 10, 1802, the Duke of Kent arrived in Gibraltar as its newest governor. After observing the deteriorated state of the garrison posted to the colony over the ensuing two weeks (which included the rape of two Spanish women who had come to admire the view over the bay) Edward went into action. Of the ninety wine houses at Gibraltar, the Duke closed fifty in an effort to reduce drunkenness by the soldiers under his command. Specific times were set for soldiers to drink at regimental canteens, and local pubs were ruled out of bounds. The Duke also imposed strict routine in the day-to-day lives of his men that included training, drills, parades, and attention to personal hygiene — even the length of a soldier's beard was controlled. With these spartan measures in place, order was quickly established on the Rock, but Edward may have gone too far. Rumours of the Duke's love of discipline rekindled back in England.

On Christmas Eve 1802, members of the 1st Regiment of Foot armed themselves and stormed the Duke's residence. Screaming that slaves had received better treatment than his own men, the mutineers demanded the Duke immediately leave the garrison for England. Soldiers supporting Edward immediately rallied while others joined the Royals in their revolt. The Duke was able to regain control of the situation within two days, rounding up the ringleaders and convening a court martial. Three of the thirteen men court-martialled were executed.[6]

A detailed account was sent to the Duke of York, and on March 16 Edward received a response from the King, commanding the return of his son to England to explain his actions in person. Lieutenant Governor Sir Thomas Trigge was sent to assume the reins of the colonial government, triggering a flood of letters supporting the Duke of Kent. It was expected that Edward would resign before the arrival of his replacement, but the Duke refused. When Trigge arrived at the colony he was surprised to see the Duke's personal standard still fluttering in the warm Mediterranean breeze.

Edward paraded his soldiers in front of his stunned replacement (they showed no signs of the previous mutiny). The master of the ship that brought Trigge to Gibraltar, Captain William Parker, later wrote an account of what he witnessed at the Rock that day:

> H.R.H. made a point of reviewing all the regiments before Sir Thomas [Trigge], and showing him the whole garrison, that he might be convinced of the order in which everything was on his resigning the command ... I fear the string was wound up rather too tight; but nevertheless, his enemies have made the story much worse than it is; and he says, from the neglect of the officers, he was under the necessity of taking steps he would not otherwise have done ... His judgement is sound and good, and reckoned superior to that of most of the Royal Family; but he is wrapt [*sic*] up in his profession, which he studies night and day; and his maxim is, that nothing is well when it can be better. He is a most perfect gentleman, which demands all of his acquaintances the most perfect respect, and at the same time has a reserve about him which prevents the possibility of any one becoming familiar with him.[7]

By May 27, 1803, Edward was back in England demanding to be allowed to officially explain his actions to both the Duke of York and the King, but no one wanted to hear from him. There would be no official court martial that would have allowed Edward or his supporters the chance to exonerate him. Edward tried to get the British government to involve themselves in the situation, but was informed that Cabinet had no wishes to interfere in the Duke of York's decision to advise the King to send him home. Frustrated, the Duke wrote to his brother the Prince of Wales, detailing an earlier private meeting he had with the Duke of York. "[W]e had … a very long conversation together …" Edward recounted to the Prince of Wales, "which, as you may suppose, was a very painful one to me."[8] The Duke of York had then informed his brother that he had no intention of returning him to Gibraltar and that the 1802 mutiny had been the result of Edward's harsh regulations.

A formal interview between the Duke of York and Duke of Kent was scheduled for September 13, 1803, a meeting that left Edward heartbroken — he was informally blamed for the events at Gibraltar and would not be given any chance to redeem himself. In one final act of defiance, Edward refused to resign his office as governor and commander-in-chief of Gibraltar even though he no longer had any authority in the outpost. The pay attached to the posting was promptly removed.

The following years are sad ones for Edward. Returning to Castle Hill Lodge with Julie, Edward fell into the routines of royal appearances with his family and tried to manage the debts that rapidly mounted following his unemployment. The peace created by the Treaty of Amiens had collapsed during the Duke's return voyage to England, but he would not be given an opportunity to serve his country during the ensuing war.

Napoleon Bonaparte declared himself emperor on May 18, 1804, and all Edward could do was plead with the prime minister for an appointment overseas. Always with the 1802 mutiny at the back of his mind, Edward wrote to William Pitt on October 20 asking to be returned to Gibraltar, in case Spain entered the war on the side of France. Edward argued that he deserved the chance to wipe the stain of Gibraltar off his professional record, and that the prime minister was his only hope to be "actively employed in that quarter where I have been so peculiarly unfortunate."[9] Nothing came of the Duke's request.

In 1804, Edward would be commissioned as a field marshal (the highest rank in the British Army), but the appointment was hollow in that it carried no posting or potential for command. Instead, the Duke spent much of his time engaged in his extensive philanthropic work,[10] as well as writing lengthy letters to the Prince of Wales about the health of their father.

King George III was listing dangerously into insanity as his bouts with mental illness become more and more frequent during the opening years of the nineteenth century. Both 1801 and 1804 had been difficult years for the King, exacerbated by his absolute hatred of the Prince of Wales. The year 1804 had also been a particularly difficult one thanks to a very public spat between the Prince and Princess of Wales over custody of their only daughter, Princess Charlotte.

Prince George's mounting debts (which towered those of Edward) were a cause of real concern for the Royal family. In 1794, King George III had agreed to clear his eldest son's debts if he agreed to marry and produce a legitimate heir. The Prince of Wales agreed, marrying his first cousin, Princess Caroline of Brunswick. There are reports of Prince George being blinding drunk on his wedding night, yet the pair were still able to conceive a much needed heir. Princess Charlotte was born exactly nine months after the wedding, and her conception proved to be the last time the Prince and Princess of Wales would share a bed. Prince George quickly returned to Maria Fitzherbert, and Caroline was cast aside.

The Princess of Wales did not go quietly, but instead hosted wild parties that were breeding grounds for rumours of her own infidelities. It all came to a head when Caroline adopted an orphan named William Austin (born in 1802) who was widely believed to be an illegitimate son born to her after an affair with an admiral in the Royal Navy, Sir Sydney Smith. By 1804 the orphan was the centre of a national scandal, and two years later the Dukes of York and Clarence demanded an investigation proving the paternity of William Austin. A "Delicate Investigation"[11] was soon organized by Parliament.

Although she was eventually exonerated of being the mother of an illegitimate child, the public presentation of evidence of countless lovers, orgies, and so on, eviscerated Caroline's reputation. The Princess of Wales was banned from court and the care of her daughter was placed in the hands of the King. During the investigation it also came out that Caroline had received council from the Duke of Kent without the knowledge of the Prince of Wales, initiating an erosion of the strong relationship between the royal brothers that would never recover.

The same year that the Princess of Wales was cast from London, John Graves Simcoe (he had returned from Upper Canada due to health concerns in 1796, and since then served briefly in Haiti) was appointed to replace Charles Cornwallis, the 1st Marquess Cornwallis, as commander-in-chief of India. Edward had always wanted this prestigious appointment and rather callously wrote to the Prince of Wales on October 28, 1806, after hearing of Simcoe's declining health: "Poor Simcoe, I hear, is dying [he had actually died two days earlier at the age of 54]. Could *I* succeed *him* and get out to India for three or four years, I should esteem myself the most fortunate of men, if I am to be kept from returning with [brilliance] to the Mediterranean."[12] Ultimately, this request was also rejected, even though the appointment of Edward to India would have greatly relieved his indebtedness, now reported by the comptroller of his household to be at £108,200 (approximately £8,161,622.76 in 2012 funds, or $12,787,504.72 Canadian dollars).[13]

Throughout all of this Edward continued his regular correspondence and patronage of the de Salaberry family. Personally supporting the military careers of Louis, and Françoise-Catherine's sons Charles-Michel, Maurice-Roch, François-Louis and Édouard-Alphonse (The Duke of Kent and Madame de St. Laurent's "godson"), Edward and Julie were always ready to entertain or house them at Castle Hill Lodge or Kensington Palace. In one of his many letters detailing the progress of three of the boys to their father, Edward proudly boasted, "I will add that Maurice is fully as tall as myself, being nearly six feet two inches, that [François-Louis] is not so tall, being about five feet ten inches, and that Edward promises to be a Hercules, in short, all three are the true stuff that make excellent soldiers, and I can vouch for their success."[14]

Edward's letters to the de Salaberrys also touched on events going on back in Canada, and in particular, the Duke's opinions of the various appointments being made to the colonies. In 1807 Edward expressed his approval of the appointment of General Sir James Henry Craig as governor general and commander-in-chief. In fact, General Craig hand-delivered a letter on behalf of the Duke to Louis de Salaberry affirming, "I have seized the opportunity to name you to [Craig] as one of the Canadian subjects of His Majesty whom I most esteem, and in whom I take a lively interest, and I have every reason to believe, from the assurances which he has given me, that you will be one of the first objects of his attention, as I have requested him to arrange for you in some way."[15] Edward goes on to say, "I have seen … a letter which I received from Mr. Dunn [civil administrator of British North

America before the arrival of Craig] himself, that he has recommended your appointment to the Executive Council, and I have no doubt that after a little while, I shall have the satisfaction of knowing, that the new chief has added a place in the Legislative Council, when we will be able to say *'the victory is ours.'*"[16] In 1808, Louis de Salaberry was appointed surveyor for the preservation of woods and timber for Lower Canada and, by 1817, he was given a seat in the Legislative Council for Lower Canada.

Governor General Sir James Henry Craig was a popular choice for the British living in Canada, although the man was near death when he arrived in Quebec. After taking his oath of office in bed at Chateau St. Louis, Craig gradually recovered but struggled with chronic dropsy (swelling due to the accumulation of fluid in body tissue) during his nearly four years on the continent. Aligning himself with the pro-English elements within Canadian society (which included Edward's friends Jonathan Sewell and Louis de Salaberry) Craig immediately came into conflict with the largely French Lower Canadian Assembly.

Craig's interactions with the Assembly — and his habit of favouring the English minority of Lower Canada — prompted the publication of the French-language newspaper *Le Canadian* in 1806. *Le Canadian*'s writers, most notably Pierre Bédard, began to publish radical statements such as "the first duty of this House [of Assembly] … was to maintain its independence even against the attempts by the first branch, [i.e. the executive] to lessen it,"[17] directly attacking the role of the Crown in government. Craig responded to such writings, as well as the expulsion of a close friend, Ezekiel Hart, from taking his seat in the legislature because he was Jewish, by dissolving the Assembly in May 1809. Learning of the events through Louis de Salaberry, Edward responded by writing back to his friend saying, "your Governor General did well in acting with firmness … for it would not be prudent to permit any opposition to the representative of the Sovereign."[18]

Edward's comment on the supremacy of the Crown in British North American politics is important to note. Whether his statement was informed by his knowledge of the uneasy balance within Canada that required the stability afforded by the Crown, or by the fact that Craig's actions had been supported by such friends of the Duke as Jonathan Sewell (by then chief justice of Lower Canada, as well as speaker of its Assembly) is unknown. Regardless, in the era before responsible government, Edward's belief in the supremacy of the Crown was consistent with his previous notions of the Sovereign as a unifying force.

With his health in rapid decline by 1811, Sir James Henry Craig was barely able to get back to England in time to die there on January 12, 1812. With his return to Britain, the office of governor general and commander-in-chief was again up for grabs and Edward wanted it.

The political climate in Britain had changed dramatically by 1811. King George III had plunged into permanent madness after the death of his favourite daughter, Amelia (the princess died after contracting measles on Edward's 44th birthday). Within four months of Amelia's death, the "Care of King During his Illness, etc. Act" was passed declaring the Prince of Wales Regent (King in all but name). George III deteriorated into a feeble, blind old man shuffling around his apartments at Windsor Castle while the Prince Regent relished his new powers and the income that came with them.

In North America there were increasing signs that the United States saw the remaining northern colonies of Britain as ripe for conquest. The British policy of impressment (forcing captured American sailors to serve in the Royal Navy), restricting United

States' trade in Europe, and supporting First Nations in their fight along the northwestern frontier pushed American politicians (called War Hawks) in the direction of war. By 1812, American President James Madison would famously declare that the invasion of Canada would be "a mere matter of marching."

Up until 1811, the Duke of Kent had been lobbying the government to appoint him commander-in-chief of the King's Mediterranean Forces (which would have included Gibraltar), a position that did not yet exist. Writing to Sir John McMahon, private secretary to the Prince Regent, on March 15, 1811, about his great hopes for work in the Mediterranean, the Duke added a postscript:

> I believe I need not mention (as it is well understood) that, in point of *finance*, employment abroad at this moment that would add to my income would be a matter of very great accommodation to me, and therefore that, altho' nothing would be so repugnant to my wishes as returning to North America, I should think twice before I declin'd even *that* offer, in the event of my fond hopes & anxious expectations of the Mediterranean command being disappointed.[19]

Unfortunately, there was little interest in sending Edward overseas again in the service of King and country. Realizing his dream of returning to the Mediterranean was not to be, Edward experienced a change of heart concerning British North America. Writing to Sir John McMahon ten days later, the Duke of Kent submitted:

> I of course am compelled to turn my thoughts,
> from the peculiarity of my situation, to the pro-
> posal once suggested by the Prince [Regent] to
> me of the Governor Generalship [*sic*] of British
> North America, and the Chief Command of
> his forces in those parts, and notwithstanding
> the extreme objection I have to the severity of
> the Canadian climate, and the immense dis-
> tance of that station from hence, to state that I
> should now wish to be informed of the footing
> on which it is intended to offer those situations
> to me.[20]

Edward's warming to the idea of a Canadian posting is emphasized in his unannounced visit to Colonel J.W. Gordon, (quartermaster-general to the forces — a senior general) the same day he had written to McMahon requesting the governor generalship. Edward talked to the surprised general for a half-hour about Canada and the Prince Regent's plans to send him there, prompting Gordon to send his own letter to McMahon detailing the bizarre visit.[21]

That the Duke of Kent could have been governor general during the War of 1812 presents some very interesting scenarios. The energy and attention to detail (regardless of budgetary constraints) Edward demonstrated during his time as commander-in-chief in Nova Scotia offer a window into how he may have conducted the North American war. Unfortunately for the Duke, we will never know. On October 21, 1811, Sir George Prevost (a man who took an immediate disliking to Edward's meddling in North America) was appointed as Craig's replacement. That the Duke's defences, including his telegraph system, would deter the United States from attacking the harbour at

Halifax were of little consolation.

The reason for Edward again being overlooked can only be speculated. Clearly the warm relationship that he had once enjoyed with the Prince Regent had cooled considerably (highlighted by the fact that his letters were now being addressed to Prince George's private secretary and not the Regent directly), possibly due to Edward's actions during the "delicate investigation" of Princess Caroline.

Added to Edward's disappointment of not even being allowed back to Canada, there came the crushing news that both Maurice-Roch and François-Louis de Salaberry had died, having fallen victim to disease while serving the Crown in India. Édouard-Alphonse's death would follow in 1812 when the young soldier was killed during the storming of Badajoz in Spain. Writing to Charles-Michel, the only surviving son of Louis and Françoise-Catherine de Salaberry, after the loss of his brother, Edward reassured his friend and protégé "that since the commencement of your troubles, none of you have been for an instant absent from [Julie and my] thoughts."[22] The Duke's letter also contained news that he had been successful in securing a promotion for Charles-Michel as a lieutenant-colonel, as well as a commission creating the young soldier superintendent of the Canadian Voltigeurs (a light infantry regiment of French Canadians loyal to the Crown). A constant source of aggravation for the Duke of Kent, Governor General Prevost would only issue Charles-Michel a militia rank (making his station inferior to someone in the regular British Army). Still, Lieutenant-Colonel de Salaberry proved to be an excellent recruiter, creating a disciplined and professional militia corps.[23]

When the War of 1812 was officially declared, the Duke of Kent could only wait for reports to cross the Atlantic to learn of new developments. However, whenever news about Charles-Michel and his well-disciplined Canadian Voltigeurs made its way back to England, Edward must have felt a twinge of pride. A great supporter of the British and Canadian efforts against the invading American armies, the Duke of Kent wrote to Charles-Michel on August 8, 1813:

> In general, all you tell me of the appearance of things in your vicinity, as to the present campaign, is extremely cheering, and I look forward with some degree of confidence to a succession of comfortable accounts from Canada during the remainder of the season. I have been doing all I can here to impress the necessity of doubling your number of seamen on the lakes, and sending you out a couple of thousand Highlanders yet this season; but I am not able to say whether my counsel will be attended to or not.[24]

The essence of one of the Duke of Kent's pet projects during his time as commander-in-chief (creating a Canadian corps that could be dispatched anywhere on the continent) was employed during the War of 1812. While they remained separate regiments, the Royal Newfoundland Fencibles, Royal Nova Scotia Fencibles, and the New Brunswick Regiment all served in Upper Canada. The lack of soldiers in Upper and Lower Canada necessitated augmentations from the other colonies, and undoubtedly the Duke used these examples to further his idea for a unified Canadian regiment that would not be restricted to serve in one specific province or colony. If British North America was going to survive in the face of American aggression, Edward argued, its regiments would have to be willing to serve anywhere within its vast boundaries.

It was during the mid-point of the war that the Duke of Kent's lobbying efforts on behalf of Charles-Michel bore fruit. In the fall of 1813, an American army of 4,000 troops commanded by Major-General Wade Hampton approached Montreal from the south after crossing the Lower Canadian frontier from New York State. When an advance party of 1,500 American soldiers confronted 460 Canadian Voltigeurs under the command of Charles-Michel de Salaberry on October 26, the Battle of Châteauguay erupted along the banks of the river of the same name. Holding a good defensive position in the woods and heroically led by Charles-Michel, the Canadian militia (90 percent of whom were French Canadian) and Mohawk allies routed the Americans, preventing an invasion of Montreal and Lower Canada.

Still resistant to acknowledging Edward's wise recommendation of Charles-Michel as commander of the Voltigeurs, Governor General Prevost, who arrived after the battle was essentially over, issued a general order praising de Salaberry's superior officer Major-General Abraham Ludwig Karl von Wattenwyl (who also arrived late to the battlefield) for his brilliant defence against the American Army. That von Wattenwyl had only toured the defences after they had been built by Charles-Michel incensed the men. Protests by de Salaberry and others saw a revised general order released on November 4, 1813, stating: "The undaunted gallantry displayed by six companies, almost to a man, composed of Canadians, Fencibles and Militia, under the immediate command of Lieut. Col. De Salaberry, in repelling with disgrace an American invading army twenty times their number, reflects unfading honor on the Canadian name."[25]

The Duke of Kent wanted more for his protégé, and took it upon himself to ensure that Charles-Michel de Salaberry was honoured as "the hero who saved Lower Canada" (echoing Sir Isaac Brock's anointment as the "Hero of Upper Canada"). Writing to Louis de Salaberry, Edward assured his friend that "I have talked the matter over with the Duke of York, and he appears completely convinced that to your son belongs the whole merit; and I have no doubt he will find occasion to reward him in a manner appropriate to his desire and merit."[26] Thanks to Edward's lobbying, Charles-Michel was recognized for his leadership along the Châteauguay River, and Prevost was forced to recommend the French Canadian for the lucrative posting of inspecting field officer of militia in 1814.

While the governor general did issue a letter advancing de Salaberry's name, he added a supplementary note explaining that the lieutenant-colonel had only been following von Wattenwyl's orders — effectively discrediting Charles-Michel's role in the battle. Prevost's letter ensured that Charles-Michel would be passed over for the appointment, and in response the young officer resigned. Luckily for de Salaberry, the Duke of Kent prevented the resignation from going through, thus ensuring that his protégé would continue to receive a salary as a lieutenant-colonel. In 1816, de Salaberry received a medal commemorating his efforts at Châteauguay, and on June 5, 1817, he was made a companion of the Order of the Bath (the fourth most senior British order of chivalry. The Duke of Kent had been made a knight of the order — along with his brothers — by the Prince Regent two years earlier).[27]

The War of 1812 created heroes for the British North American colonies, and awoke many to the idea that they could unite into a broader union. That Maritimers served in Upper

Canada and French Canadians acted to preserve the Crown of King George III emphasized the reality of some common ground within the vast territories of British North America. Conversations about uniting the disparate colonies began across the continent, and the Duke of Kent was very much a part of them, particularly through his written correspondence with his long-time friend Jonathan Sewell.

An ardent Loyalist, Jonathan Sewell had known Edward ever since he, Jonathan, was a young lawyer and playing violin with the Royal Fusiliers during their time in Quebec (Sewell even composed new verses to "God Save the King" that were performed back in London).[28] As a member of the bar, Sewell was very protective of the Crown's royal prerogative, believing that a strong monarchy was one of the few things uniting the British North American colonies, a view he shared with both Lord Dorchester and the Duke of Kent. By 1795 Sewell had been appointed attorney general and advocate general in Lower Canada and was working to promote the authority of the Crown in his province.

Sewell's work often challenged land claims by First Nations (who seldom had the physical treaties to back their territorial claims) and the rights of French Canadians (he subscribed to the belief that if Canada was to survive it must be converted entirely into an English province). In 1808, Sewell was appointed chief justice of Lower Canada, taking a seat in the province's Executive Council and becoming the second most powerful official in the colony, after the governor general.

When called to the Legislative Council, Sewell became its speaker in 1809. In 1810, the governor general, Sir James Henry Craig, asked Sewell to examine British North America for areas that divided the region and hindered a sense of unity within its inhabitants. Replying to the governor general, Sewell's recommendations were simple and direct, laying the foundations of great conflict in the colonies and foreshadowing the Lower and Upper Canadian Rebellions of 1837–38. "The great links of connection between a Government and its subjects are religious, Laws and Language," Sewell asserted, explaining that such relationships did not exist in the colony. British and French Canadians nurtured a "national antipathy," and since no "incorporation of two such Extremes can ever be effected," the Speaker concluded, "the Province must be converted to an English Colony, or, it will ultimately be lost to England."[29]

Initially, the British government did not agree with Sewell's recommendations, and Sir George Prevost, Craig's replacement as governor general in 1811, also rejected them. In 1814, Sewell was impeached by the Legislative Assembly, citing that the rules and practices he had laid out as speaker constituted legislation and therefore could be interpreted as an attempt by the judiciary to infringe on the independence of the elected representatives. Sewell and his family immediately left for England, where he learned that the Colonial Office would not pursue any of the claims laid by the Assembly on their former speaker. All of his procedures would be exonerated and republished. This discovery ignited criticism of Prevost's administration, and the governor general was recalled one year later.

Jonathan Sewell had been surprised by the heroic actions of Charles-Michel de Salaberry and the Canadian Voltigeurs in the defence of the British Crown during the War of 1812, and he became further convinced that British North America could be unified. This belief — including a softening of his stance on the assimilation of French Canadians in this union — put Jonathan Sewell on the same footing as his old friend the Duke of Kent. Sewell's plan for a federal union (co-authored with

John Beverley Robinson, attorney general of Upper Canada, and entitled *A Plan for a General Legislative Union of the British Provinces in North America)*, explained: "It appears necessary to adopt a course which will tend to consolidate the interests and the strength of the provinces; because no hopes of effectual resistance can be entertained, unless the strength of the provinces collectively (if required) can be wielded at any time …"[30]

Lamenting the lack of control that the Crown had over the provinces, which handled their affairs as insular jurisdictions, Sewell advocated a union centred on a powerful Crown with provincial officers appointed by the governor general and largely independent of the local assemblies. Sewell's vision was not a democratic one (responsible government had not yet emerged) and relied heavily on the creation of a unified Canadian militia (an idea shared by the Duke of Kent). The proposals offered by Sewell detail a blueprint for the Confederation that would take place fifty years later. Foreshadowing 1867, Sewell wrote in 1814:

> I propose also to constitute an United Provincial Parliament, the Lower House to be formed by a delegation of Members from each of the Assemblies in the five provinces, selected by themselves; the Upper House by a selection of members from the legislative councils of each province, summoned by writ under the Great Seal of the United British Provinces, and the hand of the Governor General; the Governor General constituting the third branch, and to this superior provincial legislature, I propose to give power to enact laws for the welfare and good government of the United British

Provinces, in all matters of general interest, that is to say, of general interest, in reference to the United British Provinces collectively.[31]

Acknowledging the receipt of Sewell's plan, the Duke of Kent wrote back to his friend:

> [N]othing can be better arranged than the whole thing is, or more perfected; and when I see an opening it is fully my intention to hint the matter to Lord Bathurst [British Secretary of State for War and the Colonies], and put the paper into his hands, without however telling him from whom I have it, though I shall urge him to have some conversation with you relative to it.[32]

The Duke also commented on some aspects of Sewell's proposal and suggested slight changes to the planned union.

Edward's critiques centred on reducing the provinces of British North America to two: one encompassing the Canadas and the other the Maritimes. His recommendations are consistent with his belief in the role of the governor general as intrinsically important to the unity of the region as a new political jurisdiction. By reducing the number of lieutenant governors, Edward may have been trying to avoid the regional power struggles that he had witnessed between the governor general and strong-willed provincial representatives of the King, such as John Graves Simcoe and William Waldegrave. Indeed, in geographical terms, Edward's "two province" model would have been more balanced (using the 1814 boundaries).

Following the 1837–38 Rebellions in Upper and Lower Canada, the *Report on the Affairs of British North America* was issued by John Lambton, Lord Durham, who spent five months on the continent after the crisis. The significance of this report is twofold: the first was that it reprinted the Duke of Kent's letter to Sewell in an attempt to justify the unification of the two Canadas (one of Edward's ideas). The other significance is that Durham's report was laid in front of the reigning monarch, Queen Victoria, Edward's daughter.

Lord Durham appealed to the Queen in his report:

> The views on which I found my support of a comprehensive union have long been entertained by many persons in these Colonies, whose opinion is entitled to the highest consideration.... Mr. Sewell, the late Chief Justice of Quebec, laid before me an autograph letter addressed to himself by Your Majesty's illustrious and lamented father, in which his [*sic*] Royal Highness was pleased to express his approbation of a similar plan then proposed by that gentleman. No one better understood the interests and character of these Colonies than his [*sic*] Royal Highness; and it is with peculiar satisfaction, therefore, that I submit to Your Majesty's perusal the important document which contains his Royal Highness's opinion in favour of such a scheme.[33]

That Edward's name was being evoked to his daughter in an appeal to unite the colonies of British North America (however disastrous the joining of Upper and Lower Canada proved to be) places the Duke of Kent at the very heart of Canada's constitutional development as a unified state. Kent's name gave weight to Sewell's and Lord Durham's proposals, and would be cited again during the Charlottetown and Quebec Conferences of 1864 (precursors to Confederation three years later). When the four original colonies finally united in 1867, they did so under the Crown of Victoria — whom John A. Macdonald, the new dominion's first prime minister, called the "Queen of Canada."[34] This title would see formal realization when it was granted to Queen Elizabeth II by the *Act Respecting the Royal Style and Titles* of 1953.

The extraordinary developments that would result in Edward's daughter becoming the "Mother of Confederation"[35] followed the tragic death of the Prince Regent's only legitimate child, Princess Charlotte Augusta of Wales, during her delivery of a stillborn son in 1817. By then the Duke of Kent had moved to Brussels in yet another effort to try and curb spending (before leaving he had surrendered half of his income to a committee that had been formed to pay down his debts). Quietly living with the ever-faithful Julie de St. Laurent, Edward suddenly found himself at the centre of a succession crisis. With the death of Princess Charlotte, no legitimate heir remained for the House of Hanover — a staggering fact considering King George III and Queen Charlotte had thirteen children who survived into adulthood.

A rash of weddings ensued as the royal dukes attempted to produce legal offspring, and Edward was obliged to follow suit. With the family dynasty at stake, the Duke of Kent separated from his mistress of twenty-seven years, marrying the sister of Princess Charlotte's widowed husband, Princess Victoria of Saxe-Coburg-Saalfeld, first in Amorbach, Leiningen, and then again at a joint ceremony in England with the Duke of Clarence marrying Princess Adelaide of Saxe-Meiningen. Now alone, Julie de St. Laurent would be financially supported by the Duke until his death. Numerous letters remain highlighting the continued love Edward felt for his former mistress. Retiring to live with her sister in Paris, Julie died in 1830. The city was engulfed in yet another revolution that saw Edward and Julie's friend, Louis Philippe, proclaimed King of the French the day before her burial in the Cimetière du Père-Lachaise.

By November 18, 1818, the Duchess of Kent was pregnant and Edward was eager to return to England so that the potential heir to the throne could be born on British soil. Penniless, Edward solicited a £10,000 bond from the committee that oversaw his income, and appealed to his brother (undoubtedly widening the rift between them) to have the former apartments of Princess Charlotte readied for the arrival of his pregnant wife.

With the renovations of Charlotte's apartments at Kensington Palace still going on around them, the Duke and Duchess of Kent became the parents of a daughter at 4:15 a.m. on May 24, 1819.[36] Edward was genuinely delighted and fawned over his baby girl. Animosity between the Duke and the Prince Regent now reached new heights as it seemed very likely that this child would eventually ascend the throne. Prince George refused to set a date for the baby girl's christening, and reserved the right to name the child himself.

Edward had intended to name his daughter Georgiana (after the Prince Regent), Charlotte (after his mother), Augusta (after one of Edward's sisters), Alexandrina (after the baby's godfather the Tsar of Russia), and Victoria (after her mother). When Prince George finally announced a date for the christening (giving the family only three days' notice), he waited until the night before the event to make his decision known about the names put forward by Edward: All would be vetoed except Alexandrina.

"[T]he name of Georgiana could not be used, as He did not chuse [*sic*] to place the name before the Emperor of Russia's, and he could not allow it to follow," explained the Regent's private secretary Sir Benjamin Bloomfield. During the actual christening, the Prince Regent unexpectedly announced that he would also veto any names of the current Royal family. When the Archbishop of Canterbury cautiously asked what names the child was allowed to have, Prince George would only agree to that recognizing the Tsar of Russia. The Archbishop insisted on a second name, and even though the Duke of Kent offered "Elizabeth," the Prince Regent blurted out, "Give her the mother's name also then, but it cannot precede that of the Emperor." Thus, the child was finally christened "Alexandrina Victoria," and known to her family as "Drina." When writing to Sir John Wentworth the day after the christening, Edward did not use the names selected by the Prince Regent, poignantly referring to his daughter as only "the infant." Once the child learned to write, she quickly assumed her second name, becoming Princess Victoria — the name she preferred.

Sadly, the Duke of Kent would have less than a year to spend with his daughter. Leasing Woolbrook Cottage in Sidmouth, Devon, an area of England with weather that Edward said reminded him of Canada, the Duke and Duchess settled into domestic country life. However, they both contracted colds in the cold and wet January weather, with the Duke's developing into pneumonia accompanied by uncontrollable vomiting and a high fever. As was common practice at the time, doctors applied leeches to Edward's chest and head in their misguided attempt to alleviate his symptoms (heated cups were also used to draw out the blood). All told, nearly a gallon of blood was removed from the Duke of Kent over the next few days.

Mercifully, on January 23, 1820, Prince Edward Augustus, Duke of Kent and Strathearn, died at Woolbrook Cottage at the age of fifty-two. His final words were recorded as, "May the Almighty protect my wife and child, and forgive all of the sins I have committed," before he turned to his wife, saying, "Do not forget me."[34] Six days later, the tortured shell of King George III followed his son.

The Duke of Kent was interred in the Royal Vault of St. George's Chapel at Windsor Castle on February 11, 1820. His tomb was placed alongside those of his younger brothers, Princes Alfred (died 1782) and Octavius (died 1783), whose remains had been moved there from Westminster Abbey the day before. Edward's father, the much loved or loathed (depending on which side of the Atlantic, or end of North America, you were on) King George III was entombed nearby on February 16. The King rests beside his wife, Queen Charlotte, to whom he had always been faithful.

Edward's brother ascended the throne as King George IV, and was crowned in an opulent ceremony (many commented that the King resembled a rather fat bird of paradise) at Westminster Abbey the following year. George IV's estranged consort Caroline literally had the door slammed in her face (after bayonets were held to her chin) when she tried to attend the coronation. Caroline began feeling sick the very evening after her spectacle at the coronation, and three weeks later died of either an intestinal obstruction, cancer, or even poisoning (no one really knows). Caroline's body was returned to her ancestral home in the Duchy of Brunswick for burial, her coffin bearing an inscription identifying her as the "injured queen of England."

No longer the handsome figure he had been in his youth, King George IV's appearance reflected years of overindulgence. Once the leader of British fashion and high society, George's silhouette now resembled that of a pear. No longer trusted (George IV was notorious for changing political allegiances whenever it suited him, or his pocketbook), the King was hopelessly addicted to the laudanum used to shore up his rapidly deteriorating health. Ultimately, King George IV had little time to enjoy the title he had coveted for so long.

Isolating himself at Windsor Castle for his final years, George IV spent his time recounting great victories he had at the Battle of Waterloo (a battle he did not attend) and designing grand buildings that would never see the light of day. On June 26, 1830, the peacock King died, much to the relief of England and her empire. The pomposity that marked the life and reign of George IV came to an abrupt end as the Crown passed to George III's third son (his second son Prince Frederick died in 1827), the sixty-nine-year-old Prince William Henry, Duke of Clarence.

Prince William's earlier escapades in Canada, in particular his birthday celebrations off the coast of Newfoundland, accurately reflect the nature of the man. William had been waiting for the Crown ever since the death of his older brother Frederick. Determined to outlive George IV, William gargled two gallons of seawater a day and wore rubber boots to ensure his feet were always dry. A simple man, old "Coconut Head" wasted little time claiming his birthright. Upon hearing of his brother's death, King William IV raced through London in an open carriage, grinning ear to ear, bowing to anyone who would look at him (even letting the local prostitutes kiss his hand) and offering his new subjects a lift. "Who is Silly Billy now?"[37] the new King quipped as the Privy Council assembled to swear their allegiance.

The coronation of King William cost only a tenth of that for his older brother, and signalled the establishment of a much more frugal court. A crude man (he had a habit of spitting copiously in public), William did not get along with the ambitious widow of the Duke of Kent. William's legion of illegitimate children had no claim to the throne (all of the King's legitimate children died within three months of being born), meaning that Edward's daughter was the heir presumptive.

The Duchess of Kent was well aware of her daughter's destiny, particularly since Princess Victoria would be considered a minor (allowing her mother much influence over decisions of state) until her eighteenth birthday. William and the Duchess fought bitterly over young Victoria, both circulating explicit stories about each other's sexual exploits. During his seventy-first birthday dinner the King exclaimed, in the presence of the Duchess of Kent and his seventeen-year-old niece, that he hoped he would live to see Princess Victoria turn eighteen, thus ensuring that her mother would have no influence over the Crown. Coconut Head got his wish and died one month after Victoria's birthday, paradoxically muttering "The church, the church."[38]

While the Lower and Upper Canadian Rebellions (1837–38) were erupting across the sea in British North America, the Imperial Crown fell to the eighteen-year-old niece of the King. Victoria, daughter of the Duke and Duchess of Kent, became Queen of the world's largest empire on June 20, 1837. It was the birth of the Victorian Era, a period of history that would also see the creation of, in words written by the Queen herself in her personal diary, "The Great Confederation of British North America … under the new name of Canada."[39]

On June 11, 1879, Princess Louise (daughter of Queen Victoria and granddaughter of Prince Edward, Duke of Kent)

Detail from the portrait of a young Queen Victoria that hangs in the Canadian Senate, artist, John Partridge (1786–1872). This painting was damaged in the 1849 burning of the Montreal Parliament buildings (a reaction to the Union Act of 1841 that saw the implementation of Lord Durham's controversial 1838 report). The portrait had to be rescued again when the original Parliament Buildings at Ottawa burned down in 1916.

was invited by her husband, the Marquess of Lorne and governor general of the Dominion of Canada, to lay the cornerstone for "Kent Gate" at Quebec City. Part of a larger restoration project initiated by the previous governor general, Lord Dufferin, after he blocked local businessmen's attempts to demolish the walls surrounding the old city, the Kent Gate was one of the jewels of a project that also included "Dufferin Terrence." In fact, an earlier cornerstone had been laid by Lord Dufferin in October of 1878, but the governor general had requested that the official pronouncement of the gate's name be held until Princess Louise's arrival in Canada the following spring.

Placing a leaden box in the cornerstone filled with artifacts of the time (including English shillings bearing the effigy of Queen Victoria supplied by Louise), the Princess covered the stone with mortar using a silver-handled trowel. Nearby stood the city engineer, Charles Baillairgé, whose grandfather François had worked on interior decoration of the cathedral of Notre-Dame in Quebec while Prince Edward resided in the city.

Photo by Roy and Greta Vanderwal.

Kent Gate allows Rue Dauphine access through the ramparts to the old section of Quebec City. This was the first gate to be restored when it was decided in the 1870s not to pull down the ancient walls of the city. Princess Louise, granddaughter of Prince Edward, laid the foundation stone of this gate in 1879.

Queen Victoria herself partially funded and followed the construction of Kent Gate, an enduring reminder of her father's time in the old city, as well as of his love for French Canada. If only, shivering in the cold of his first Canadian winter at Quebec City, Edward could have foreseen seventy years later that his daughter would become Queen of a vast Dominion that ultimately grew to encompass all of the northern part of the continent.

The irony surrounding Queen Victoria's (the daughter of a man who spent much of his time on this continent in exile from his family) first audience with her Canadian prime minister is hard to ignore. John A. Macdonald, bowing low to his Queen, explained that the purpose of Confederation, born in the tiny capital of the island that bore her father's name,[40] was "to declare in the most solemn and emphatic manner our resolve to be under the Sovereignty of Your Majesty and your family forever."

Appendix A:

Offspring of King George III (1738–1820) and Queen Charlotte (1744–1818) of the House of Hanover

Prince George Augustus Frederick, Prince of Wales, Duke of
   Cornwall and future King George IV (1762–1830)
Prince Frederick Augustus, Duke of York and Albany
   (1763–1827)
Prince William Henry, Duke of Clarence and future
   King William IV (1765–1837)
Princess Charlotte Augusta Matilda, Princess Royal (1766–1828)
Prince Edward Augustus, Duke of Kent and Strathearn
   (1767–1820)
Princess Augusta Sophia (1768–1840)
Princess Elizabeth (1770–1840)
Prince Ernest Augustus, Duke of Cumberland and future
   King of Hanover (1771–1851)
Prince Augustus Frederick, Duke of Sussex (1773–1843)
Prince Adolphus Frederick, Duke of Cambridge (1774–1850)

Princess Mary, Duchess of Gloucester and Edinburgh
(1776–1857)
Princess Sophia Matilda (1777–1848)
Prince Octavius (1779–1783)
Prince Alfred (1780–1782)
Princess Amelia (1783–1810)

Appendix B:

Key Figures During Prince Edward Augustus, Duke of Kent's Association with Canada (1790–1820)

In the United Kingdom:

Sovereign   His Majesty King George III (1760–1820)
(His Royal Highness the Prince Regent 1811–1820)

Prime Minister   William Pitt the Younger (1783–1801)
Henry Addington (1801–1804)
William Pitt the Younger (1804–1806)
William Wyndham Grenville, 1st Lord
     Grenville (1806–1807)
William Cavendish-Bentinck, 3rd Duke of
     Portland (1807–1809)
Spencer Perceval (1809–1812)

Robert Banks Jenkinson, 2nd Earl of
    Liverpool (1812–1827)

Home Secretary	William Wyndham Grenville, 1st Lord Grenville (1789–1791)
	Henry Dundas, 1st Viscount Melville (1791–1794)
	His Royal Highness the Duke of Portland (1794–1801)
	Thomas Pelham, 2nd Earl of Chichester (1801–1803)
	Charles Philip Yorke (1803–1804)
	Robert Banks Jenkinson, 2nd Earl of Liverpool (1804–1806)
	George John Spencer, 2nd Earl Spencer (1806–1807)
	Robert Banks Jenkinson, 2nd Earl of Liverpool (1807–1809)
	Richard Ryder (1809–1812)
	Henry Addington, 1st Viscount Sidmouth (1812–1822)
War Secretary (becomes Secretary of State for War and the Colonies in 1801)	Henry Dundas, 1st Viscount Melville (1794–1801)
	Robert Hobart, 4th Earl of Buckinghamshire (1801–1804)
	John Jeffreys Pratt, 1st Marquess Camden (1804–1805)
	Robert Stewart, 2nd Marquess of Londonderry (1805–1806)
	William Windham (1806–1807)

Robert Stewart, 2nd Marquess of
Londonderry (1807–1809)
Robert Banks Jenkinson, 2nd Earl of
Liverpool (1809–1812)
Henry Bathurst, 3rd Earl Bathurst (1812–
1827)

Commander-in-chief of the Forces	Field Marshal Henry Seymour Conway (1782–1793)
	General Jeffery Amherst, 1st Lord Amherst (1793–1795)
	His Royal Highness Prince Frederick, Duke of York (1795–1809)
	General Sir David Dundas (1809–1811)
	His Royal Highness Prince Frederick, Duke of York (1811–1827)

In British North America:

Governor General and Commander-in-chief of British North America	Guy Carleton, 1st Lord Dorchester (1786–1796)
	Robert Prescott (1796–1807)
	*His Royal Highness Prince Edward, Duke of Kent appointed commander-in-chief (1799–1802)
	Sir James Henry Craig (1807–1811)
	Sir George Prevost, 1st Baronet (1812–1815)
	Sir John Coape Sherbrooke (1816–1818)
	Charles Lennox, 4th Duke of Richmond and Lennox (1818–1819)

George Ramsay, 9th Earl of Dalhousie
(1820–1828)

Lieutenant Governor of Upper Canada (after 1791)	John Graves Simcoe (1792–1796) Peter Hunter (1799–1805) Francis Gore (1806–1817) Sir Peregine Maitland (1818–1828)
Lieutenant Governor of Lower Canada (after 1791)	Sir Alured Clarke (1790–1793) Robert Prescott (1796–1797) Sir Robert Milnes (1799–1805) Sir Robert Burton (1808–1832)
Lieutenant Governor of Nova Scotia	John Parr (1786–1791) Sir John Wentworth (1791–1808) Sir George Prevost (1808–1811) Sir John Coape Sherbrooke (1811–1816) George Ramsay, 9th Earl of Dalhousie (1816–1820)
Lieutenant Governor of New Brunswick	Thomas Carleton (1786–1817) George Stracey Smyth (1817–1823)
Lieutenant Governor of the Island of St. John (renamed Prince Edward Island in 1799)	Edmund Fanning (1787–1805) Joseph Frederick W. DesBarres (1805–1812) Charles D. Smith (1813–1824)

Lieutenant Governor of Cape Breton Island	William Macarmick (1787–1815)
	George Robert Ainslie (1816 until colony was reunited with Nova Scotia in 1820)

Governor of Newfoundland	Mark Milbanke (1789–1792)
	Sir Richard King (1792–1794)
	Sir James Wallace (1794–1797)
	William Waldegrave (1797–1800)
	Sir Charles M. Pole (1800–1801)
	James Gambier (1802–1804)
	Sir Erasmus Gower (1804–1806)
	John Halloway (1807–1809)
	Sir John T. Duckworth (1810–1813)
	Sir Richard Godwin Keats (1813–1816)
	Sir Francis Pickmore (1816–1818)
	Sir Charles Hamilton (1818–1824)

Appendix C:

The Canadian Legacy of Prince Edward Augustus, Duke of Kent

The coat of arms used by the province of Prince Edward Island (officially known as "The Queen's Arms in Right of Prince Edward Island") were first granted by King Edward VII in 1905. The upper section of the shield bears a gold lion passant on a red background — a design taken from the arms of Prince Edward Augustus, Duke of Kent.

1. Quebec

The Duke of Kent Tournament and Trophy, Royal Quebec Golf Club

Kent Course, Royal Quebec Golf Club

Kent House, Quebec City, home of Prince Edward from 1791–1794, and currently the residence of the French Consulate in Quebec

Kent House, Montmorency Falls

Kent Gate, Quebec City, built in 1879, and partially funded by Queen Victoria, to honour the Duke of Kent's residence in Quebec

Rue du Duc-de-Kent, Quebec City

Rue du Duc-de-Kent, Beauport

Rue Kent, Gatineau

Rue Kent, Longueuil

Rue Kent, Sainte-Anne-de-Bellevue

Rue du Prince-Édouard, Quebec City

2. Nova Scotia

Castle Hill Drive, named after an English residence in Ealing, West London, purchased by the Duke of Kent from Maria Fitzherbert in 1800

Chain Rock Drive, Halifax, named after an iron ring left-over from a chain Prince Edward ordered slung across Bedford Basin as part of its defences

Edwardsville, Cape Breton Island

Julie's Walk, Halifax, named after Madame de St. Laurent

Kent Avenue, Halifax

Kent Park, Halifax

Kent Street, Halifax

Kentville, King's County, named in 1826 after a vote by the inhabitants to honour a 1794 visit by the Prince

Lodge Drive and Lodge Crescent, Halifax, named after the Prince's Lodge

Martinique Beach, Halifax, Prince Edward took part in the 1794 Capture of Martinique

Point Edward, Cape Breton Island, named in the 1790s

Prince Edward Trail, Hemlock Ravine Park, Halifax

Prince's Lodge and Hemlock Ravine, Halifax

Prince's Walk, Halifax

St. Laurent Place, Halifax

3. Ontario

Kent Street, Ottawa, originally called Hugh Street, it was renamed after the Duke of Kent in the late nineteenth century

Prince Edward County

Prince Edward Street, Brighton

Point Edward Village

Township of Edwardsburgh/Cardinal, established January 1, 2001, by the amalgamation of Edwardsburgh Township with the Village of Cardinal

4. New Brunswick

Kent County

Kent Junction

Kent Lake

Prince Edward Street, Saint John

Prince Edward Square, Saint John

Telegraph Hill, named after the telegraph system set up by the Duke of Kent between Halifax and Fredericton

5. Prince Edward Island

The legislature of St. John's Island voted to change the island's name to Prince Edward Island in honour of Prince Edward on November 29, 1798. The Act received Royal Assent by King George III on February 2, 1799, and came into effect on June 3, 1799.

Kent College, established in 1804 by Lieutenant Governor Edmund Fanning and his Legislative Council, the college would eventually become the University of Prince Edward Island, Charlottetown

Kent Street, Charlottetown

Chronology of Prince Edward

circa 1742
March: Joseph Brant is born in the Mohawk Valley.

1750
Population of New France is 50,000; the Thirteen Colonies 1,200,000; Newfoundland is 7,000.

1752
February 25: John Graves Simcoe is born in Cotterstock, England.

July 4: Louis de Salaberry is born in Beauport, Quebec.

1754
Beginning of the French and Indian Wars (the Seven Years' War, 1754–1763).

His Royal Highness, The Prince Edward Augustus, Duke of Kent and Strathearn, Earl of Dublin (1767–1820)

British North America, Canada, and the World

April 17: Battle of Culloden, British forces massacre the Scottish Jacobite followers of Bonnie Prince Charlie. Scotland becomes part of the United Kingdom.

1755
July 10: Pierre de Rigaud de Vaudreuil de Cavagnial, Marquis de Vaudreuil, is proclaimed governor general of New France, becoming the first "Canadian-born" vice-regal representative in Canadian history.

December 9: Canada's first post office opens in Halifax.

1756
May 13: Louis-Joseph de Montcalm, Marquis de Montcalm, arrives in New France to take command of all land forces stationed in the territory.

1757
Montcalm is made commander-in-chief of all forces in New France, and given authority over Governor General Vaudreuil.

1758
July 26: Fortress Louisbourg

His Royal Highness, The Prince Edward Augustus, Duke of Kent and Strathearn, Earl of Dublin (1767–1820)	*British North America, Canada, and the World*

surrenders to British forces under Major-General Jeffery Amherst.

October 2: First meeting of the Nova Scotia Legislative Assembly — the first popularly elected Parliament in Canada.

1759
September 12–14: Battle of the Plains of Abraham ensues as British Major-General Wolfe attacks the citadel at Quebec. Within ten minutes the battle was won by the British forces. Montcalm leaves the citadel to engage the British and is mortally wounded in the stomach and thigh. Wolfe is hit three times, succumbing to his wounds on the battlefield. Montcalm dies the following morning.

1760
The population of New France is 64,041.

September 8: Articles of Capitulation are signed in Montreal by Governor General Vaudreuil, surrendering New France to the British Crown. Frederick Haldimand takes possession of the city for the British.

His Royal Highness, The Prince Edward Augustus, Duke of Kent and Strathearn, Earl of Dublin (1767–1820)

British North America, Canada, and the World

October 25: King George III assumes the throne after the death of his grandfather, King George II.

1761
James Cook begins surveying Halifax Harbour (will finish in 1762).

1762:
May 16: 200 English settlers arrive in New Brunswick from Massachusetts to become the first British residents of the province.

September 12: Catherine the Great is crowned as empress in Moscow, Russia.

September 22: Elizabeth Posthuma Gwillim (the future wife of John Graves Simcoe) is born in Whitchurch, Herefordshire.

1763
James Cook begins surveying and mapping coastlines of Newfoundland and Labrador.

February 10: The Treaty of Paris is signed, confirming New

His Royal Highness, The Prince Edward Augustus, Duke of Kent and Strathearn, Earl of Dublin (1767–1820)

British North America, Canada, and the World

France as a territory of King George III. French habitants who did not switch their allegiance to George III were free to leave – only 270 did. Province of Quebec (with Quebec City as its capital) is created out of the conquered lands of New France.

October 7: King George III issues his Royal Proclamation in British North America limiting westward expansion by the Thirteen Colonies and placing First Nations under the protection of the Crown.

circa 1764
Thérèse-Bernardine de Montgenêt (Edward's Julie de St. Laurent) is born in Besançon, France.

June 6: Jonathan Sewell is born in Cambridge, Massachusetts.

August 10: Civil government begins in the Province of Quebec with James Murray appointed as first governor of Quebec.

1765
March 8: The Stamp Act passed by the British Parliament,

His Royal Highness, The Prince Edward Augustus, Duke of Kent and Strathearn, Earl of Dublin (1767–1820)

British North America, Canada, and the World

upsetting American colonist who must now affix stamps on various documents (including playing cards and dice).

1767
November 2: Prince Edward Augustus is born in London to Queen Charlotte and King George III. He was their fifth son.

1767
July 23: St. John's Island (Prince Edward Island) broken into parcels and assigned, by lottery, to 100 lords, military officers, politicians, high-ranking civil servants, wealthy merchants, and business adventurers.

1768
November 1: Sir Guy Carleton becomes governor of Quebec (he had already been in the colony for two years as acting lieutenant governor of Quebec).

1769
September 19: Walter Patterson arrives on St. John's Island as its first governor.

1770
March 5: The first clash between American colonists and the British Army happens outside the Boston Customs House. This will be recorded as the Boston Massacre, one of the first steps toward the American Revolution.

His Royal Highness, The Prince Edward Augustus, Duke of Kent and Strathearn, Earl of Dublin (1767–1820)

British North America, Canada, and the World

1773
July 3: St. John's Island's first Assembly meets at the Crossed Keys Tavern in Charlottetown.

December 16: The Boston Tea Party — 342 chests of tea are thrown into the Boston Harbor to protest the British monopoly over tea sales in North America.

1774
June 22: The Quebec Act is passed by the British Parliament. Roman Catholics in the province are granted religious freedom and French civil law is reestablished. Americans record this piece of legislation as one of the "Intolerable Acts" that led them to revolution.

September 5: First Continent Congress of American Colonies meets in Philadelphia. Declaration of Rights and Grievances is drawn up to counter Quebec Act.

1775
April 19: The first shots of the American Revolution are fired at Lexington and Concord, Massachusetts.

His Royal Highness, The Prince Edward Augustus, Duke of Kent and Strathearn, Earl of Dublin (1767–1820)	*British North America, Canada, and the World*

May 10: Second Continental Congress meets in Philadelphia.

June 15: George Washington selected by Congress as commander-in-chief of an American Continental Army.

June 24: Nova Scotia House of Assembly promises Britain that the province will remain loyal to the Crown.

November 17: Charlottetown attacked and pillaged by American privateers.

1776
April 1: Fleeing violence in the Thirteen Colonies, 1,124 United Empire Loyalists arrive in Halifax.

June: Joseph Brant personally presents land grievances to King George III in London.

July 4: The American Continental Congress issues the Declaration of Independence.

1777
June 26: Sir Guy Carleton resigns as governor of Quebec,

His Royal Highness, The Prince Edward Augustus, Duke of Kent and Strathearn, Earl of Dublin (1767–1820)

British North America, Canada, and the World

succeeded by Sir Frederick Haldimand.

October 15: While fighting American rebels in North America, John Graves Simcoe takes command of the Queen's Rangers.

1778
British Governor John and Frances Wentworth flee New Hampshire for England.

Spain and France become allies of the American Colonies against the British Crown.

March 29–April 26: James Cook charts coast of British Columbia along with George Vancouver.

November 19: Charles-Michel de Salaberry is born in Beauport, Quebec.

1780
Joseph Brant is given a captaincy in the British Army.

1781
October 19: British General Cornwallis surrenders at

His Royal Highness, The Prince Edward Augustus, Duke of Kent and Strathearn, Earl of Dublin (1767–1820)

British North America, Canada, and the World

Yorktown, Virginia, ending the Crown's campaign against the American colonists.

1782
Sir John Johnson appointed "superintendent general and inspector general of the Six Nations Indians and those in the Province of Quebec."

May: Sir Guy Carleton is sent to New York City to oversee evacuation of 30,000 British troops and 27,000 refugees fleeing the new American republic — 1,200 will be settled near Halifax.

1783
John and Frances Wentworth arrive in Halifax, Nova Scotia, after the former was appointed surveyor general.

Summer: Joseph Brant appeals to First Nations' leaders to repel American advances westward into North America. Brant's proposals are supported by the British Crown.

August: Black Loyalists arrive in Shelburne, Nova Scotia. Many

*His Royal Highness, The Prince
Edward Augustus, Duke of Kent
and Strathearn, Earl of Dublin
(1767–1820)*

**British North America, Canada,
and the World**

are former slaves from the
United States.

September 3: With the signing
of the Treaty of Paris, the
British Crown recognizes the
independence of the United
States of America. The last British
troops are evacuated by Sir Guy
Carleton from New York City.

1784
May 22: A large number of
United Empire Loyalists land
at the Bay of Quinte (settling
present-day Kingston, Ontario).

June 18: New Brunswick is
created from the colony of
Nova Scotia as more and more
Loyalists flood into the region.
Thomas Carleton is appointed
colony's first governor.

August 26: Cape Breton Island
separates from Nova Scotia.

1785
The Northwestern War erupts
between various First Nations
and the United States of America
over control of the Northwestern
Territories.

His Royal Highness, The Prince Edward Augustus, Duke of Kent and Strathearn, Earl of Dublin (1767–1820)	British North America, Canada, and the World

May 18: Parrtown, New Brunswick, becomes the first incorporated city in British North America. It is later renamed Saint John.

1786

Prince Edward is sent to continental Europe to train as a soldier.

Prince Edward is invested as a member of the Order of the Garter by his brother Prince Frederick in Hanover, Germany.

1786

October 13: Sir Frederick Haldimand departs Quebec and Sir Guy Carleton (now Lord Dorchester) replaces him as governor general and commander-in-chief of British North America.

October: As captain of HMS *Pegasus*, Prince William Henry tours British North America. The Prince turns 21 off the coast of Newfoundland (resulting in raucous celebrations at sea), and pays frequent visits to Frances Wentworth in Halifax.

1787

King George III suffers his first bout of "madness" (likely caused by the genetic disease porphyria).

April 15: The English-speaking Loyalist population of Quebec petitions the British government for a British-style colony in the Upper St. Lawrence region (present-day Ontario).

His Royal Highness, The Prince Edward Augustus, Duke of Kent and Strathearn, Earl of Dublin (1767–1820)

British North America, Canada, and the World

August–September: Prince William Henry tours the Province of Quebec as far west as Montreal.

September 17: The American Constitution is approved at a convention presided over by George Washington at Philadelphia.

1788
Louis de Salaberry marries Françoise-Catherine Hertel de Rouville.

1789
Prince Edward is appointed colonel of the Royal Fusiliers (7th Regiment of Foot).

Prince Edward enters the Masonic Order while in Geneva, Switzerland.

December 15: While in Geneva, Switzerland, Prince Edward's affair with musician Adelaide Dubus results in the birth of illegitimate daughter Adelaide Victoire Auguste (the infant died the following year as she sailed with her aunt from Marseilles to Gibraltar to be reunited with Edward).

1789
November 9: Lord Dorchester confers the hereditary postnominals "U.E." (standing for "Unity of the Empire") to all American Loyalists who immigrated to British North America following the American Revolution (before 1783).

June: The Estates-General is dissolved in France, signalling the beginning of the French Revolution.

July 14: French revolutionaries storm the Bastille fortress in Paris.

His Royal Highness, The Prince Edward Augustus, Duke of Kent and Strathearn, Earl of Dublin (1767–1820)

British North America, Canada, and the World

August 26: The French National Assembly publishes the *Declaration of the Rights of Man and of the Citizen.*

1790

A disgraced Prince Edward arrives, unannounced, back in London. Within a month King George III had sent his son to Gibraltar.

November 23: Julie de St. Laurent arrives in Gibraltar and becomes the companion of Prince Edward.

December 13: Prince Edward writes to King George III requesting to be posted to Quebec.

1791

August 11: Prince Edward (and Julie de St. Laurent) arrives in Quebec.

Prince Edward meets Jonathan Sewell, a young lawyer who begins playing violin with the Royal Fusiliers regimental band.

December 26: The Constitution Act dividing the Province of Quebec into Upper and Lower Canada is proclaimed by Lord

1790

Rumours begin circulating around London that John Graves Simcoe will be appointed the first lieutenant governor of Upper Canada.

1791

Population of Lower Canada is 160,000. Population of Upper Canada is 14,000.

March 4: Vermont becomes the 14th state in the United States of America.

June 10: British Parliament passes

His Royal Highness, The Prince Edward Augustus, Duke of Kent and Strathearn, Earl of Dublin (1767–1820)

British North America, Canada, and the World

Dorchester in Quebec City. Prince Edward witnesses the event and attends celebrations throughout the settlement.

the Canada Act (or Constitution Act), the first time "Canada" is used to identify the territory encompassed by the old Province of Quebec. Quebec is ordered to be divided into two provinces named Upper Canada (present-day Ontario) and Lower Canada (present-day Quebec). The Act is proclaimed on November 18 to take effect on December 26.

September: France is declared a constitutional monarchy.

November 11: John Graves and Elizabeth Simcoe arrive in Quebec City in preparation for their journey to Upper Canada.

1792
June 22: Prince Edward is installed as provincial grand master of Lower Canada by the Antients' faction of the Masonic Order.

June 27: During a riot outside a polling station in Charlesbourg Prince Edward calms the crowd, using the term "Canadian" to

1792
May 14: John Wentworth is appointed lieutenant governor of Nova Scotia.

September 20: France is declared a republic.

June 8: Newly appointed Lieutenant Governor John

His Royal Highness, The Prince Edward Augustus, Duke of Kent and Strathearn, Earl of Dublin (1767–1820)	*British North America, Canada, and the World*

mean both the King's French and English subjects in Canada.

July 2: Edouard-Alphonse de Salaberry is christened in Quebec with Prince Edward and Julie de St. Laurent as his godparents.

August–September: Prince Edward tours Upper Canada, visiting nearly all of its Loyalist settlements and military outposts.

August 20: Prince Edward arrives in Newark, Upper Canada, as a guest of Lieutenant Governor Simcoe. Before being received in the tiny capital, the Prince tours Fort Niagara (on the American side of the Niagara River). In Newark, Edward is met by a delegation of First Nations' Peoples who give him the name "Chief-Above-All-Other-Chiefs."

December 17: Prince Edward attends the opening of the Lower Canadian Legislature.

1793
September 4: The Quebec Sunday Free School, a non-denominational school, is

Graves Simcoe, and his wife Elizabeth, depart Quebec for Upper Canada.

July 16: John Graves Simcoe officially swears in his executive at St. George's Church in Kingston.

July: Gun-shot Treaty concluded between Lieutenant Governor Simcoe and assembled First Nations at Kingston, Upper Canada.

September 17: Upper Canada's first Parliament is opened by Lieutenant Governor Simcoe at Navy Hall in Newark (Niagara-on-the-Lake).

1793
August 27: Lieutenant Governor Simcoe establishes the settlement of York (present-day Toronto).

His Royal Highness, The Prince Edward Augustus, Duke of Kent and Strathearn, Earl of Dublin (1767–1820)

British North America, Canada, and the World

established by Prince Edward in Quebec City.

Settlement named after Prince Frederick, Duke of York.

November 10: A fire breaks out on Rue Sault au Matelot in Quebec's lower town that Prince Edward personally helps extinguish.

Autumn: A planned uprising by the Royal Fusiliers stationed in Quebec is uncovered. Quickly subdued, the soldiers involved are punished — mutineer Joseph Draper (sentenced to death) is dramatically pardoned by Lower Canada's lieutenant governor after being lobbied by Prince Edward.

July 9: *An Act Against Slavery* is introduced by Lieutenant Governor Simcoe and passed in the Upper Canadian Parliament. This begins the process of phasing out slavery in the province — the first legislation of its kind in the British Empire.

January 21: French King Louis XVI is beheaded by French revolutionaries. Queen Marie Antoinette would follow her husband to the guillotine on October 16.

May 31: The Parliament of Upper Canada passes the *Alien Act,* which guards against anti-British sentiment in the province.

Fall: Originally supporting the revolution, Louis Philippe, Duc d'Orléans, flees France. Soon after, his father is guillotined by French revolutionaries. Philippe will eventually end up in the United States.

His Royal Highness, The Prince Edward Augustus, Duke of Kent and Strathearn, Earl of Dublin (1767–1820)

British North America, Canada, and the World

1794

January 22: Prince Edward enters the United States, becoming the first member of the Royal family to visit the country since it severed its ties with the Crown. Edward was on his way to Boston to catch a ship to the Caribbean campaign of the French Revolutionary Wars. During the crossing of Lake Champlain, Edward's sleigh carrying his wardrobe breaks through the ice and is lost.

March 4: Prince Edward arrives in Martinique.

May 10: After a victorious tour in the Caribbean, Prince Edward arrives to his new posting at Halifax, Nova Scotia. The Prince's arrival touches off a golden age for the settlement.

June: Prince Edward tours Nova Scotia and New Brunswick, travelling as far as Fredericton.

August: HMS *Westmoreland* arrives in Halifax with both Julie de St. Laurent (who had been in England waiting out Edward's service in the Caribbean) and

His Royal Highness, The Prince Edward Augustus, Duke of Kent and Strathearn, Earl of Dublin (1767–1820)

British North America, Canada, and the World

news that the Prince has been appointed commander-in-chief of His Majesty's forces in Nova Scotia and New Brunswick. Edward and Julie take up residence at the Lodge (the Wentworth's country retreat outside of Halifax).

November: Prince Edward presents a report to War Secretary Henry Dundas advocating extensive fortification of the Halifax Harbour and settlement. Work begins immediately and transforms the community into the largest British military base in North America.

1795

Prince Edward establishes a telegraph system connecting Fort George to his lodgings outside of Halifax. This system will eventually be extended to connect Halifax to Fredericton, New Brunswick, by 1798.

The ship carrying Prince Edward's new wardrobe (to replace the one lost to Lake Champlain in 1794) is captured by the French Navy.

1795

John Wentworth granted a baronetcy by King George III.

April 8: In exchange for King George III clearing his debts, the Prince of Wales marries Princess Caroline of Brunswick.

July: The Second Maroon War (the first was concluded by peace treaty in 1739) breaks out in Jamaica between the Trelawny Town Maroons and British colonial government. When the Maroons sued for peace

His Royal Highness, The Prince Edward Augustus, Duke of Kent and Strathearn, Earl of Dublin (1767–1820)

British North America, Canada, and the World

five months later, the British demanded their surrender by January 1, 1796. Most did not submit by this date and were deported to Nova Scotia.

December 23: Lieutenant Governor Simcoe orders the construction of Yonge Street north to Lake Simcoe.

December 27: Elizabeth Simcoe records feeling an earthquake in her diary — the first recording by Europeans of such a phenomenon in North America.

1796
Another ship carrying new clothes and supplies for Prince Edward is captured by the French Navy.

July: Prince Edward personally greets 550 Maroons exiled from Jamaica after the end of the 1795–1796 Maroon War. The Prince puts them to work (with pay) on the Maroon Bastion of Halifax's Fort George.

1796
February 1: Lieutenant Governor Simcoe officially moves his capital to York (present-day Toronto).

July 1: Jay's Treaty comes into effect as Britain abandons most of the interior forts along the western frontier. A boundary commission is created to draw a border between British North America and the United States west of Lake-of-the-Woods, Upper Canada.

June 21: Lieutenant General

His Royal Highness, The Prince Edward Augustus, Duke of Kent and Strathearn, Earl of Dublin (1767–1820)

British North America, Canada, and the World

Robert Prescott arrives in North America to replace Lord Dorchester as governor general and commander-in-chief.

Prince Edward and Julie de St. Laurent spend a week touring New Brunswick.

July: The Simcoes return to England after John Graves's health begins to deteriorate.

1797
Prince Edward sends recruiters for his regiment to Newfoundland, upsetting the island's governor, Admiral William Waldegrave. An angry correspondence ensues between the two men, prompting Edward's assertion of the primacy of the office of governor general and commander-in-chief over all of British North America.

July: Prince Edward orders the construction of the Prince of Wales Martello Tower at Point Pleasant in Halifax, Nova Scotia.

1798
July 7: The Nova Scotia Council and Assembly vote to present Prince Edward with a diamond-

His Royal Highness, The Prince Edward Augustus, Duke of Kent and Strathearn, Earl of Dublin (1767–1820)

British North America, Canada, and the World

encrusted star of the Order of the Garter to show their appreciation for his work in the province.

August 8: Cantering on horseback through the streets of Halifax, Prince Edward is injured after his horse falls and rolls on top of him. By November Edward, accompanied by Julie de St. Laurent, heads to England to seek treatment for his bruised thigh.

November 29: The legislature of St. John's Island votes to change its name to Prince Edward Island in honour of Prince Edward. The Act received Royal Assent by King George III on February 2, 1799, and came into effect on June 3, 1799.

1799

April 24: Prince Edward is granted the titles Duke of Kent and Strathearn, Earl of Dublin, by King George III.

May 10: The Duke of Kent is appointed commander-in-chief of His Majesty's Forces in British North America — the counterpart to the civil office of governor general.

1799

April: Governor General Robert Prescott is recalled to London due the deterioration of his relationship with the members of his British North American council.

December 12: Napoleon Bonaparte declares himself "First Consul of France."

His Royal Highness, The Prince Edward Augustus, Duke of Kent and Strathearn, Earl of Dublin (1767-1820)	*British North America, Canada, and the World*
September 6: The Duke of Kent and Julie de St. Laurent return to Halifax, Nova Scotia.	December 17: George Washington dies.
November: Louis Philippe, Duc d'Orléans, and his brothers arrive at The Lodge, outside of Halifax, in an unannounced visit to the Duke of Kent.	

1800
Construction begins on St. George's Round Church in Halifax — a project supported by the Duke of Kent.

Frustrated with the widespread tardiness of Haligonians, the Duke of Kent orders the construction of a great clock for the settlement. The Vulliamy family of Switzerland is commissioned to make the giant timepiece.

April 8: A dog spooks the Duke of Kent's horse in Halifax, causing him to be thrown off. After being dragged some distance, Edward finally gets free of his stirrup but is badly hurt. The Duke requests to be returned to England to aid his recovery.

1800
The Union Acts of the Kingdoms of Great Britain (July 2) and Ireland (August 1) are passed, uniting the countries into the United Kingdom of Great Britain and Ireland. The union comes into effect on January 1, 1801.

| *His Royal Highness, The Prince Edward Augustus, Duke of Kent and Strathearn, Earl of Dublin (1767–1820)* | *British North America, Canada, and the World* |

June 5: The Duke of Kent lays the foundation stone for Halifax's Freemason Hall.

August 4: The Duke of Kent and Julie de St. Laurent leave Halifax and British North America permanently, setting sail for England.

1801
September–November: The Duke of Kent purchases Castle Hill Lodge at Ealing from Maria Fitzherbert.

1801
King George III suffers another bout of "madness."

March 25: Treaty of Amiens is signed, creating an uneasy peace between France and Britain.

August 21: The Duke of Kent leaves the Royal Fusiliers to become colonel of the 1st Regiment of Foot ("The Royals").

1802
April: The Duke of Kent ends his time as commander-in-chief of British North America to become governor and commander-in-chief of Gibraltar.

May 10: The Duke of Kent, with Julie de St. Laurent, arrives in Gibraltar.

December 24: Members of the 1st Regiment of Foot attempt to overthrow the Duke of Kent in

His Royal Highness, The Prince Edward Augustus, Duke of Kent and Strathearn, Earl of Dublin (1767–1820)

British North America, Canada, and the World

Gibraltar. The mutiny is quickly suppressed, but the Duke is ordered back to England to explain the situation in Gibraltar to the King in person.

1803

May 27: The Duke of Kent arrives back in England with Julie de St. Laurent. He will never return to service overseas.

October 20: The building housing the Garrison Clock of Halifax is finally completed on its spot near the top of Citadel Hill. This clock remains a major landmark for the city.

1803

April 30: Napoleon abandons his plans to recapture Canada, selling Louisiana to the United States for $15 million USD.

May 18: Hostilities resume between the British and French.

1804

Kent College, the first post-secondary educational institution in the colony, is established in honour of the Duke on Prince Edward Island.

1804

May 18: Napoleon Bonaparte is given the title "Emperor of the French" by the French Senate. He is crowned on December 2.

July 1: Haiti declares itself independent from France with Jean-Jacques Dessalines, later Emperor Jacques I, as its leader.

1805

September 3: The Duke of Kent is promoted to field marshal in the British Army, but is given no chance to command.

His Royal Highness, The Prince Edward Augustus, Duke of Kent and Strathearn, Earl of Dublin (1767–1820)

British North America, Canada, and the World

1806

The "Delicate Investigation" is undertaken in London after rumours of infidelity circulate around Princess Caroline (wife of the Prince of Wales).

1807

October: General Sir James Henry Craig arrives to assume command as governor general and commander-in-chief of British North America.

November 24: Joseph Brant dies at Burlington Bay, Upper Canada.

1808

April 7: George Prevost replaces Sir John Wentworth as lieutenant governor of Nova Scotia.

1809

Maurice-Roch de Salaberry dies in India while serving in the British Army.

1811

François-Louis de Salaberry dies in India while serving in the British Army.

February 5: The Prince of Wales becomes Prince Regent ("King

His Royal Highness, The Prince Edward Augustus, Duke of Kent and Strathearn, Earl of Dublin (1767–1820)

British North America, Canada, and the World

in all but name") as King George III descends into a state of permanent dementia.

October 9: Major-General Isaac Brock appointed administrator and commander of Upper Canadian forces.

1812
April 6: Edouard-Alphonse de Salaberry dies during the Siege of Badajoz in Spain (one of the bloodiest of the Napoleonic Wars) while serving with the British Army.

June 18: United States Congress declares war against Britain, which includes a plan to invade Canada. President James Madison declares a state of war the following day.

June 30: Upper Canada's Parliament gives American citizens 14 days to leave the province.

October 13: During the Battle of Queenston Heights Major-General Brock is killed by a sniper.

His Royal Highness, The Prince Edward Augustus, Duke of Kent and Strathearn, Earl of Dublin (1767–1820)

British North America, Canada, and the World

1813

November: The Duke of Kent proclaims the Masonic Articles of Union between the Antients and Moderns (headed by his brother the Duke of Sussex) as the two factions are formally united under the Grand Lodge of England.

1813

October 26: The Battle of Châteauguay (south of Montreal) where the Canadian militia were heroically led by Charles-Michel de Salaberry.

1814

A Plan for a General Legislative Union of the British Provinces in North America, written by Jonathan Sewell and John Beverley Robinson, is laid before the Duke of Kent who offers suggestions to perfect a union of British North America.

1814

Napoleon is captured and exiled to the Island of Elba off the western coast of Italy.

December 24: The United States and Britain sign the Treaty of Ghent, ending the War of 1812 and restoring North America to its 1783 borders.

1815

The Duke of Kent's telegraph system connecting Nova Scotia to New Brunswick falls into permanent disuse.

In an effort to conserve more money, the Duke of Kent and Julie de St. Laurent move to Brussels, Belgium, until their debts can be repaid.

1815

Napoleon returns to France to raise a new army, but is ultimately defeated by the Duke of Wellington at the Battle of Waterloo. He is exiled to the small south Atlantic island of Saint Helena.

His Royal Highness, The Prince Edward Augustus, Duke of Kent and Strathearn, Earl of Dublin (1767–1820)

British North America, Canada, and the World

1816

After being successfully lobbied by the Duke of Kent, the British government awards Charles-Michel de Salaberry a medal for his efforts during the Battle of Châteauguay.

1817

Louis de Salaberry is appointed to the Legislative Council of Lower Canada.

Charles-Michel de Salaberry is made a companion of the Order of the Bath.

November 6: The heir to the British throne, Princess Charlotte, dies in childbirth, triggering a succession crisis. The remaining sons of King George III rush to produce legitimate children.

1818

March: The Duke of Kent and Julie de St. Laurent separate as the succession crisis pushes him to produce a legitimate heir to succeed King George IV. Julie moves to live with her sister in Paris, France.

1818

November 17: Queen Charlotte dies in Surrey, England.

His Royal Highness, The Prince Edward Augustus, Duke of Kent and Strathearn, Earl of Dublin (1767–1820)

British North America, Canada, and the World

May 29: The Duke of Kent marries Princess Victoria of Saxe-Coburg-Saalfeld at Amorbach, Leiningen.

July 11: A second marriage ceremony between the Duke of Kent and Princess Victoria is conducted in England. At the same ceremony the Duke of Clarence (future William IV) is married to Princess Adelaide of Saxe-Meiningen.

1819
May 24: The Duchess of Kent gives birth to the Duke's only child, Princess Alexandrina Victoria (the future Queen Victoria).

1820
January 23: The Duke of Kent dies at the age of 52 after developing pneumonia.

1820
January 29: King George III dies and is succeeded by his eldest son who becomes King George IV.

July 20: George VI's coronation is celebrated in British North America nearly one year before it actually takes place.

October 16: Cape Breton Island is rejoined with Nova Scotia.

His Royal Highness, The Prince Edward Augustus, Duke of Kent and Strathearn, Earl of Dublin (1767–1820)	*British North America, Canada, and the World*

1821
The population of Lower Canada is 425,000; Upper Canada is 150,000; Newfoundland is 50,000; Nova Scotia is 120,000; New Brunswick is 70,000.

August 7: Queen Caroline, estranged wife of King George IV, dies.

1823:
January 1: Nova Scotia becomes the first province to issue coinage.

1828:
The first St. John's Rowing Regatta, North America's oldest sporting event, is held in Newfoundland.

March 22: Louis de Salaberry dies in Quebec.

February 27: Charles-Michel de Salaberry dies in Chambly, Lower Canada.

1830
August 8: Julie de St. Laurent dies alone in Paris at age 69.

1830
June 26: King George VI dies and is succeeded by his younger brother who becomes King William IV.

His Royal Highness, The Prince Edward Augustus, Duke of Kent and Strathearn, Earl of Dublin (1767–1820)	*British North America, Canada, and the World*

British North America, Canada, and the World

August 9: Louis Philippe, Duc d'Orléans, is crowned Louis Philippe I, King of the French, in Paris.

1837
June 20: King William IV dies and is succeeded by his niece, the Duke of Kent's daughter, who becomes Queen Victoria.

1837
May 7: 1,200 Patriotes meet in Lower Canada and elect Louis-Joseph Papineau their leader as the Lower Canada Rebellion erupts.

July 25: The Committee of Vigilance of Upper Canada is formed with William Lyon Mackenzie as its secretary. Mackenzie advocates overthrowing the British Crown in an Upper Canada Rebellion.

November 22: John Colborne, commander-in-chief of British North America, raises troops to crush the Patriotes of Lower Canada.

December 2: William Lyon Mackenzie composes a declaration of independence before leading 800 rebels to York. The resulting Battle of Montgomery's Tavern is a disaster that ends with Mackenzie fleeing to the United States.

His Royal Highness, The Prince Edward Augustus, Duke of Kent and Strathearn, Earl of Dublin (1767–1820)

British North America, Canada, and the World

December 13: Mackenzie declares the "Provisional Republic of Canada" on Navy Island (in the Niagara River). The republic is abandoned the following month and Mackenzie is arrested for violating American neutrality laws.

1838
May: John Lambton, first Earl of Durham, arrives in British North America. Appointed governor general, Lord Durham was charged with making recommendations on how British North America could avoid the violence that surfaced during the Upper and Lower Canada Rebellions.

1839
Lord Durham issues *The Report on the Affairs of British North America* in response to the 1837–38 Rebellions. Durham cites the 1814 correspondence between the Duke of Kent and Jonathan Sewell as providing royal support for a united province of Canada.

1839
November 11: Jonathan Sewell dies in Quebec City.

1840
February 10: Following recommendations made in the

His Royal Highness, The Prince Edward Augustus, Duke of Kent and Strathearn, Earl of Dublin (1767–1820)

British North America, Canada, and the World

Durham Report, the Act of Union is proclaimed, dissolving Upper and Lower Canada into one Province of Canada with a single legislature. Upper Canada becomes Canada West and Lower Canada is renamed Canada East.

1843
Louis Philippe, King of the French, hosts a royal visit by Queen Victoria to France.

1845
Louis Phillippe, King of the French, hosts another royal visit by Queen Victoria to France.

1850
January 17: Elizabeth Simcoe dies in Devon, England.

1853
Beginning of the Crimean War (ends in 1856).

1860
August: During his Royal Tour of British North America the Prince of Wales (future King Edward VII) visits Princes' Lodge near Halifax. A heart-shaped pond is constructed on

His Royal Highness, The Prince Edward Augustus, Duke of Kent and Strathearn, Earl of Dublin (1767–1820)

British North America, Canada, and the World

the site of the original enjoyed by Julie de St. Laurent. While visiting the site, the Prince of Wales collects sweetbriar to send back to Queen Victoria as a souvenir of her father's residence in Nova Scotia.

1864
During both the Charlottetown and Quebec Conferences, the Duke of Kent's 1814 correspondence with Jonathan Sewell is cited during discussions that ultimately lead to the creation of the Dominion of Canada.

1866
April–June: A series of raids along the American-British North American border are conducted by Fenians (Irish-Americans bent on the liberation of Ireland from British rule).

1867
March 8: The British North America Act passes through the British Parliament. Granted Royal Assent by Queen Victoria, the "Mother of Confederation," on March 29, the Act came into force on July 1.

| *His Royal Highness, The Prince Edward Augustus, Duke of Kent and Strathearn, Earl of Dublin (1767–1820)* | *British North America, Canada, and the World* |

1879
June 11: Queen Victoria's daughter Princess Louise lays the foundation stone of Kent Gate during the restoration of the old city walls of Quebec City.

1887
The Golden Jubilee of Queen Victoria is celebrated across the British Empire.

1897
The Diamond Jubilee of Queen Victoria is celebrated across the British Empire.

1901
January 22: After a reign of over sixty-three years, Queen Victoria dies at the age of eighty-one on the Isle of Wight.

1953:
February 11: The Duke of Kent's great-great-great granddaughter, Queen Elizabeth II, is formally given the title "Queen of Canada" by her Canadian Parliament.

Notes

Introduction

1. Yann Martel, *Beatrice and Virgil*, Toronto: Knopf, 2010, 16.

Chapter One: Fourth Son of the King, 1767

1. The notice published in the *London Gazette* reads, "This day about noon the Queen was happily delivered of a Prince. Her Royal Highness the Princess Dowager of Wales, his Grace, the Archbishop of Canterbury, several Lords of His Majesty's most Honourable Privy Council, and the ladies of Her Majesty's Bed-Chamber were present. This great Event was soon made known by the Firing of the Tower Guns. Her Majesty is, God be praised, as well as can be expected; and the young Prince is in perfect Health." *London Gazette*. London: H.M. Stationery Off. (No. 10777), October 31–November 1, 1767.

2. The 1701 Act of Succession declares "the most excellent Princess Sophia, Electress and Dowager Duchess of Hanover, daughter of Elizabeth, late Queen of Bohemia, daughter of James I, shall be next in succession to the Crown."

3. In 2004, the Harwell International Business Centre for Science and Technology (Oxfordshire, England) found that a sample of King George III's hair contained three hundred times the toxic level of arsenic. Professors

Tim Cox and Martin Warren discovered that one of the medications, James' Powder, being used to treat the King for his "madness," had significant traces of arsenic, which would have increased the frequency of his "attacks." "King George III: Mad or Misunderstood?" BBC News, July 13, 2004. See *www.bbc.com*

4. The Seven Years' War (1754–63) saw battles in Europe, North America, Central America, the West African coast, India, and the Philippines.

5. McKenzie Porter, *Overture to Victoria* (London: Alvin Redman, 1961), 8.

6. Ingrim Corbin, *Georgina; or, Anecdotes of George the Third. With a selection of Poetical Effusions and other Eulugiums on His Character, and on that of H.R.H. The Duke of Kent* (London: W. Whitmore, Paternoster Row, 1820), 15.

7. *Ibid.*, 6.

8. The disharmony between King George I and the future King George II created the conditions needed for the rise of Robert Walpole (1676–1745) as Britain's first "prime minister" (changing Parliament into what would become known today as the Westminster System).

9. Charles James Fox (1749–1806) was a vocal opponent of King George III, calling him a tyrant and even appearing in Parliament dressed in the colours of George Washington's Army — an action that was applauded by the Prince of Wales.

10. Queen Victoria, Personal Diary (Lord Esther's Typescripts, Vol. 7), September 21, 1838. © Her Majesty Queen Elizabeth II, *www.queenvictoriasjournals.org.*

11. Antonia Fraser, ed., *The Lives of the Kings and Queens of England* (London: Phoenix Illustrated, 1997), 279.

12. Sir John Fortescue, ed., *The Correspondence of King George the Third from 1760 to December 1783, printed from the original papers in the Royal Archives at Windsor Castle*, No. 4259 (London: Macmillan and Co., 1927), 317.

13. A. Aspinall, *The Later Correspondence of George III, 1783–1793*, Vol.1 (Cambridge: University Press, 1962), 382.

14. Archives of Nova Scotia, 2002-045/006 2, Jean Donald Gow, "HRH Prince Edward, Duke of Kent: Father to Victoria," (Halifax: n.p., 1991), 30.

15. Royal biographer Antonia Fraser notes, "This story was put about by a page who had been dismissed from the royal service so its veracity must be questionable." Antonia Fraser, ed., *The Lives of the Kings and Queens of England*, 281–82.

16. Cecil Woodham-Smith, *Queen Victoria: Her Life and Times, 1819–1861*, Vol. 1 (London: Hamish Hamilton, 1972), 8–9.

17. Stanley Weintraub, *Victoria: An Intimate Biography* (New York: Truman Talley Books, 1987), 36–37.

18. Mollie Gillen, *The Prince and His Lady* (London: Sidgwick & Jackson, 1979), 13.

19. A. Aspinall, *The Correspondence of George Prince of Wales,* Vol. II (London: Cassell, 1964), 61.

20. An interesting account of Prince William Henry's visit to Quebec City can be found in the journal of Sir Thomas Byam Martin (the captain's servant to Prince William Henry on board HMS *Pegasus*): "It gave great interest to our visit to the Canadian metropolis to find that the Governor-General [*sic*], Lord Dorchester, had, as Colonel Carlton, served under Wolfe as quartermaster-general. This interest was greatly heightened by a notification of the general's intention to have a sham fight, in order to exhibit to the Prince the movements of both armies immediately preceding and at the battle on the Plains of Abraham on the ever memorable 13th of September, 175[9]." Sir Richard Vesey Hamilton, ed., *Letters and Papers of Admiral of the Fleet Sir Thos. Byam Martin, G.C.B.* (London: Navy Records Society, 1898), 104.

21. In August 1819, Sir William Edward Perry named Byam Martin Island in Nunavut, Canada, after Sir Thomas Byam Martin.

22. A "bumper" refers to a drinking vessel filled to the brim. William Dyott offers this anecdote after a night of drinking with the Prince: "His Royal Highness, whenever any person did not fill a bumper, always called out, 'I see some of God Almighty's daylight in that glass, Sir; banish it.'" Reginald W. Jeffery, *Dyott's Diary 1781-1845: A Selection From the Journal of William Dyott, sometime General in the British Army and aide-de-camp to His Majesty King George III* (London: Archibald, Constable and Company, 1907), 46.

23. Hamilton, ed., *Letters and papers of Admiral of the Fleet Sir Thos. Byam Martin, G.C.B.* (London: Navy Records Society, 1898), 36.

24. Reginald W. Jeffery, ed. *Dyott's Diary 1781-1845: A Selection from the Journal of William Dyott,* 36–60.

25. John Wentworth (1737–1820) was the Harvard-educated former governor of colonial New Hampshire from 1767–75. Born in Portsmouth, New Hampshire, Wentworth came from a prominent family in the colony (his grandfather had been a lieutenant governor of New Hampshire). While at Harvard, Wentworth became friends with John Adams (second president of the United States) and was even an official spokesman for New Hampshire against the Stamp Act in 1765. John Wentworth, married his cousin, Frances Deering Wentworth on October 28, 1769. John Wentworth was appointed lieutenant governor of Nova Scotia after the death of Colonel John Parr in 1791.

26. Jeffery, *Dyott's Diary 1781-1845: A Selection From the Journal of William Dyott,* 37.

27. *Ibid.*
28. *Ibid.*, 42–43.
29. Thomas Raddall, *Halifax: Warden of the North* (Halifax: Nimbus Classics, 2010), 99.

Chapter Two: Exiled to the Rock, 1791

1. B. Cornwell, *A Description of Gibraltar: with an account of the block-ade, siege, the Attempt by Nine sail of Fire-Ships, the Sally made from the Garrison, and every Thing remarkable or worthy Notice that has occurred in that Place since the Commencement of the Spanish War: Likewise The vast importance of this valuable Fortress to Great Britain clearly stated and explained* (London: Richardson and Urquhart, 1782), 4.
2. *Ibid.*, 46.
3. The Regiment remained in Gibraltar until 1791. On October 14, 1959, The Queen's Royal Regiment was amalgamated with the 1st Battalion The East Surrey Regiment to form 1st Battalion The Queen's Royal Surrey Regiment.
4. "Fusiliers" was the accepted spelling of the word by 1751.
5. The policy of numbering British regiments this way was abandoned in 1881 under the Childers Reforms, and the name was again changed to "The Royal Fusiliers (City of London Regiment)." In 1968, the regiment was amalgamated with The Royal Northumberland Fusiliers, The Royal Warwickshire Fusiliers, and The Lancashire Fusiliers to become The Royal Regiment of Fusiliers.
6. H.L. Wickes, *Regiments of Foot: A Historical Record of All the Foot Regiments of the British Army* (Southampton, UK: Camelot Press, 1974), 11–13.
7. The colours are now on display at New York's West Point Military Academy.
8. Theodore P. Savas and J. David Dameron, *A Guide to the Battles of the American Revolution* (New York: Savas Beatie, 2010), XXXVI.
9. Roger Fulford, *Royal Dukes* (London: Collins, 1973), 165–66.
10. John Williamson, *The Elements of Military Arrangement, and of the discipline of war; adapted to the practice of the British infantry,* Vols. 1–2 (London: Medicine, Science and Technology, 1791), 153.
11. *Ibid.*, 171–72.
12. Roger Norman Buckley, *The British Army in the West Indies: Society and the Military in the Revolutionary Age* (Gainesville: University Press of Florida, 1998), 206.
13. Williamson, *The Elements of Military Arrangement, and of the discipline of war,* 162.
14. W. Wheater, *Historical Record of The Seventh or Royal Regiment of Fusiliers* (Leeds: F.B. Guerin, 1875), 81.

15. *Ibid.*
16. A. Aspinall, *The Later Correspondence of George III, 1783–1793,* Vol. 1 (Cambridge: University Press, 1962), 507.
17. *Ibid.,* 507–08.
18. Calpe is an ancient name for Gibraltar.
19. Wheater, *Historical Record of The Seventh or Royal Regiment of Fusiliers,* 82.
20. A. Aspinall, ed., *The Correspondence of George, Prince of Wales, 1770–1812,* Vol II (London: Cassell, 1964), 74.
21. Royal Archives, e-mail message to author, July 31, 2012.
22. Wallis Simpson (June 19, 1896–April 24, 1986) was the mistress of King Edward VIII (June 23, 1894–May 28, 1972). Edward VIII abdicated the throne of the British Empire in 1936, after reigning for less than one year so he could marry her. The abdication of King Edward VIII led to the accession of King George VI, father of the present Queen Elizabeth II.
23. McKenzie Porter, *Overture to Victoria* (London: Alvin Redman, 1961), 72.
24. Porter may have learned about Julie de St. Laurent's fictitious habitation of Montmorency Falls from Joan E. Morgan's popular history *Castle of Quebec,* which explores the story of Quebec City. Joan E. Morgan, *Castle of Quebec* (Toronto: J.M. Dent and Sons, 1949), 104–06.
25. As quoted in Mollie Gillen, *The Prince and His Lady* (London: Sidgwick & Jackson, 1970), 12–22.
26. Sir John Wentworth to John King, May 8, 1794. Public Archives of Nova Scotia, 2002-045/009, #22.
27. Malaga is located in Andalusia, Spain, approximately sixty-two miles (one hundred kilometres) east of Gibraltar. There is no record of how the bankrupt Marquis de Permangle made it to this location.
28. Mollie Gillen, *The Prince and His Lady,* 34.
29. A municipality on Île d'Orléans continues to be called Saint-Laurent-de-l'Île-d'Orléans.
30. John Catanzariti, ed., *The Papers of Thomas Jefferson, vol. 20,* (Princeton: Princeton University Press, 1990), 478.

Chapter Three: Quebec, 1791

1. Jean Donald Gow, "HRH Prince Edward, Duke of Kent: Father to Victoria," unpublished manuscript, 1991, 175. Held at Archives of Nova Scotia, 2002-045/006 2.
2. Aspinall, *The Later Correspondence of George III,* 557.
3. Gow, "HRH Prince Edward, Duke of Kent: Father to Victoria," 94.
4. Today, the office of the governor general of Canada claims Samuel de Champlain as the first governor general of Canada.

5. The role of intendant, created by King Louis XIV in 1663, was one of the three components of the Royal Government of New France, the other two roles being the governor and the sovereign council. The intendant controlled the civil administration of the colony, and was second in rank to the governor. The ruins of the Intendant's Palace were rediscovered in 1971 and can be visited as a tourist attraction in today's Quebec City.

6. The governor's residence was eventually destroyed by a fire in 1834, and its ruins demolished in 1892 in preparation for the construction of the Canadian Pacific Railway's Château Frontenac and the surrounding boardwalk, known today as "Dufferin Terrace."

7. Born in 1718 in Yverdon, Switzerland, Frederick Haldimand joined a regiment of the Swiss Guards in the Dutch Army in 1745. Jacques Prevost, a former Swiss officer in the French Army, encouraged the British government to form a regiment in 1755 by blending professional soldiers from various foreign armies with German and Swiss settlers in Pennsylvania, and deploy them to fight against the French Crown in North America. Frederick Haldimand became an officer in this new regiment and fought in the North American campaign of the Seven Years' War (1756–63). Haldimand was appointed "Captain General and Governor-in-Chief [*sic*] in and over our Province of Quebec in America" in 1778 and remained in office until 1786. His time in office coincided with the American Revolution and resettlement of the Loyalists, including First Nations' allies. Appointed as a knight to the Order of the Bath in 1785, Sir Frederick Haldimand died in Yverdon on June 5, 1791.

8. Known as Château St. Louis, the former residence of the French governors of New France was originally built in 1648 by Charles Huault de Montmagny. A second château, built on the site in 1694 by Governor Louis de Buade, Comte de Frontenac, was heavily damaged during the siege of Quebec in 1760. It was destroyed by fire in 1834, and the site of the château is now occupied by the Château Frontenac and Dufferin Terrace.

9. Mary Quayle Innis, *Mrs. Simcoe's Diary* (Toronto: Macmillan of Canada, 1965), 41–42.

10. Dr. John Mervin Nooth was baptized September 5, 1737, in Sturminster Newton, England, and died on May 3, 1828, in Bath, England. With the outbreak of the American Revolution, Nooth was appointed both physician extraordinary and purveyor in the medical service of the British Army in North America. He returned to England after the 1783 Treaty of Paris. Later that year he was sent to Quebec as the superintendent general of hospitals and became doctor to Prince Edward Augustus in 1791. It was Dr. Nooth whom Prince Edward sent for after falling from a horse in 1798 (see Chapter 6).

11. Public Archives of Nova Scotia, Dr. John Mervin Nooth, Letter to Sir Joseph Banks, January 2, 1792, Jean Donald Gow Fonds. It is also worth noting that Colonel E.A. Cruikshank uncovered a 1791 account published by P. Campbell, speculating on the existence of a volcano in Upper Canada (near present-day Hamilton) : "Here I was told of a phenomenon which surprises everybody in the neighbourhood, supposed to be a volcano which makes at certain times a loud report, resembling a great gun at a distance. The Indians only know the spot in which it is and from a foolish notion, or tradition among them, will not discover it; they suppose it is occasioned by the Great Spirit and how soon the white people find it, they are to be extirpated from the land if not from the face of the earth, and an end put to their race." Colonel E.A. Cruikshank, "Notes on the History of the District of Niagara, 1791–1793," Pamphlet # 26 (1913?), 12, published by the Niagara Historical Society.

12. Mary Quayle Innis, *Mrs. Simcoe's Diary*, 44.

13. Born in Kent, England, on January 2, 1727, James was the son of a distinguished general, Lieutenant General Edward Wolfe.

14. From proclamation issued by His Excellency John G. Simcoe in 1796, quoting Dorchester's original proclamation. Held by the National Archives of Canada, FC3070 L6 U62 1796 fol.

15. Earle Thomas, *Sir John Johnson: Loyalist Baronet* (Toronto: Dundurn Press, 1986), 139.

16. Brigadier General E.A. Cruikshank, ed., *The Correspondence of Lieut. Governor John Graves Simcoe, with allied documents relating to his administration of the government of Upper Canada*, Vol. 1 (Toronto: Ontario Historical Society, 1923), 55.

17. Frederick Haldimand to John Johnson, May 17, 1784. Quoted in Thomas, *Sir John Johnson*, 114.

18. The Huron-Iroquois Wars (mid-seventeenth century) resulted in the destruction of the Wyandot (Huron) and Neutral First Nations of southern Ontario.

19. Cruikshank, "Notes on the History of the District of Niagara, 1791–1793," 14.

20. Gillen, *The Prince and His Lady*, 40.

21. Dorothy Twohig, *The Journal of the Proceedings of the President, 1793–1797* (Charlottesville: University Press of Virginia, 1981), 69.

22. Lord Dorchester's last plea for a united government under the British North American provinces under a strong governor general was made in 1793. Quoting Paul David Nelson, "His reasons for reintroducing this subject were a desire to rein in Simcoe and a conviction that such a governmental organization for Canada was the soundest." Paul David Nelson, *General Sir Guy Carleton, Lord Dorchester: Soldier-Statesman of Early*

British Canada (Madison, WI: Fairleigh Dickinson University Press, 200), 215.

23. The island changed its name to Prince Edward Island, in honour of Prince Edward, Duke of Kent, on November 29, 1798.

24. This act, passed by the British Parliament after they realized that the French culture in North America would not be assimilated into British Society, expanded the political boundaries of Quebec from the banks of the St. Lawrence to encompass the whole of British North America (excluding the Maritimes and lands of the Hudson's Bay Company) and preserved French civil law, the Roman Catholic Church, and the seigniorial system.

25. Aspinall, *The Later Correspondence of George III*, 576.

26. Paul David Nelson, *General Sir Guy Carleton, Lord Dorchester: Soldier-Statesman of Early British Canada*, 211.

27. Mary Beacock Fryer and Christopher Dracott, *John Graves Simcoe, 1752–1806: A Biography*, (Toronto: Dundurn Press, 1998), 34.

28. *Ibid.*, 34–35.

29. Royal Archives, Colonel John Graves Simcoe to Henry Dundas, June 1, 1791, RA GEO/MAIN/681S-6822. Reproduced with the permission of Her Majesty Queen Elizabeth II.

30. Compound Monarchy is a political theory put forward by Dr. David Smith (Senior Policy Fellow, Johnson-Shoyama Graduate School of Public Policy) and Dr. Michael Jackson (University of Regina) that the Crown in Canada exists collectively as the Sovereign, governor general, and lieutenant governors.

31. Cruikshank, ed., *The Correspondence of Lieut. Governor John Graves Simcoe*, 61.

32. The word "cahots" referred to "bump or jolts."

33. Mary Quayle Innis, *Mrs. Simcoe's Diary*, 41.

34. Gow, *HRH Prince Edward, Duke of Kent*, 100.

35. "Manoir Montmorency Kent House" now sits on the site of the original building, which was destroyed by a fire in 1993. The reconstructed house is now part of Parc de la Chute-Montmorency, and home to a fine dining restaurant, bistro, gift shop, and interpretive centre.

36. In fact, when I started writing this book, a friend and colleague of mine at Waterdown District High School, Timothy Harvey, presented me with a family tree linking his family to the Prince through an alleged daughter, Elizabeth Guelph (date of birth unknown), born to Edward and Julie de St. Laurent while they lived in Canada.

37. See the section entitled "The Facts" in the appendix discrediting each of Edward's alleged offspring. Mollie Gillen, *The Prince and His Lady*, 266–82.

38. Gow, *HRH Prince Edward, Duke of Kent*, 94.

39. Gillen, *The Prince and His Lady*, 50.
40. Aspinall, *The Later Correspondence of George III*, Vol. 1, 853.
41. Innis, *Mrs. Simcoe's Diary*, 44.
42. Dr. William James Anderson, *The Life of F.M., H.R.H. Edward, Duke of Kent, illustrated by his correspondence with the de Salaberry Family, never before published, extending from 1791 to 1814* (Toronto: Hunter, Rose & Company, 1870), 14.
43. Arthur Bousfield and Garry Toffoli, *Home to Canada: Royal Tours, 1786–2010*, (Toronto: Dundurn Press, 2010), 33–34.
44. Mollie Gillen, *The Prince and His Lady*, 47–48.
45. It should be noted that Louis de Salaberry was elected in both Dorchester and Charlesbourg ridings, and he chose to represent the former, leaving the other seat vacant. Berthelot Dartigny was proclaimed elected by acclamation for this riding on February 18, 1793.

Chapter Four: The Royal Tour to Upper Canada, 1792

1. At the time Sir Joseph Banks was serving as president of the Royal Society of Great Britain, a position he would hold from 1778–1820.
2. Henry Scadding, *Letter to Sir Joseph Banks, (President of the Royal Society of Great Britain) written by Lieut.-Governor Simcoe, in 1791, prior to his departure from England for the purpose of organizing the new province of Upper Canada; to which is added the five official speeches delivered by him at the opening or closing of Parliament in the same province*, (Toronto: Copp Clark, 1890), 8.
3. *Ibid.*
4. Alexander Hamilton was a New York delegate to the Congress of the Confederation.
5. The Federal Convention was held from June 1 to 26, 1787.
6. Harold A. Syrett, ed., *The Papers of Alexander Hamilton*, Vol. IV, (New York City: Columbia University Press, 1966), 184–86.
7. John Catanzariti, ed., *The Papers of Thomas Jefferson*, Vol. 24, (Princeton: Princeton University Press, 1990), 607.
8. As this chapter was being written, the annual conference of lieutenant governors and territorial commissioners was being held at Rideau Hall in Ottawa. Welcoming the vice-regals to his residence, Governor General David Johnston remarked: "Each of us has been given a great responsibility. We represent the Crown — and together, we are vital to maintaining the balance of our Confederation. This fact is perhaps underappreciated in Canada today. As former Lieutenant Governor of Saskatchewan Lynda Haverstock and Dr. Michael Jackson have written: 'The genius of the Crown is that it balances the roles of Sovereign, governor general and lieutenant governor to incarnate Canada's federal and parliamentary

polity." At the heart of this balanced system is what has been termed a 'compound monarchy.' I think it is quintessentially Canadian, this idea of a shared Crown. What a wonderful symbol of unity and diversity to guide us!" Rideau Hall, June 27, 2012.

9. Quoted in William Barclay Allen and John Clement Fitzpatrick, ed., *George Washington: A Collection* (Indianapolis. IN: Liberty Classics, 1988), 446.

10. Edward Carrington was a delegate to the Congress of the Confederation from Virginia. By 1791 he had been appointed supervisor of the revenue for the District of Virginia.

11. Catanzariti, ed., *The Papers of Thomas Jefferson*, Vol. 24, 42.

12. Syrett, ed., *The Papers of Alexander Hamilton*, Vol. IV, 444.

13. Catanzariti, ed., *The Papers of Thomas Jefferson*, Vol. 24, 435.

14. Brigadier General E.A. Cruikshank, ed., *The Correspondence of Lieut. Governor John Graves Simcoe, with allied documents relating to his administration of the government of Upper Canada*, Vol. 1, (Toronto: Ontario Historical Society, 1923), 204.

15. Frank Prochaska, *The Eagle & The Crown: Americans and the British Monarchy* (New Haven: Yale University Press, 2008), 13–16.

16. Henry Scadding, *Letter to Sir Joseph Banks, (President of the Royal Society of Great Britain) written by Lieut.-Governor Simcoe, in 1791*, 7.

17. This would eventually become London, Ontario, (founded by Simcoe in 1793) and would be vetoed as the capital of Upper Canada by Lord Dorchester in favour of York (Toronto).

18. Royal Archives, Colonel John Graves Simcoe to Henry Dundas, June 1, 1791, RA GEO/MAIN/681S-6822.

19. *Ibid.*

20. George Maclean Rose, *A Cyclopedia of Canadian Men & Women: Being Chiefly Men of the Time*, (Toronto: Rose Publishing, 1886), 578.

21. Governor General Sir Frederick Haldimand granted six miles of land, called the "Haldimand Grant," on both sides of the entire length of the Grand River, to the Six Nations in recognition for their services to the Crown during the American Revolutionary Wars. Joseph Brant, a leader in the Mohawk community, was a strong advocate on behalf of the Six Nations, and lived along the Grand River before moving to the shoreline of Lake Ontario, near the location of the present-day Joseph Brant Memorial Hospital in Burlington.

22. Cruikshank, ed., *The Correspondence of Lieut. Governor John Graves Simcoe*, Vol. 1, 180.

23. Archives Ontario, Miskokomon Paper, March 24, 1927. Part of the A.E. Williams/United Indian Bands of Chippewas and Mississaugas Papers, F 4337. Cited by David T. McNab, "The Promise That He Gave To My Grand Father Was Very Sweet: The Gun Shot Treaty of 1792 at the Bay of

Quinte," *The Canadian Journal of Native Studies*, Vol. XVI, No. 2 (1996): 293–314.

24. Howard Zinn, *A People's History of the United States*, (New York: Harper, 2003), 125.
25. Cruikshank, ed., *The Correspondence of Lieut. Governor John Graves Simcoe*, Vol. 1, 168.
26. It was likely in honour of Sir George Yonge's interest in Roman road construction that Simcoe named Upper Canada's "Yonge Street" after him.
27. Cruikshank, ed., *The Correspondence of Lieut. Governor John Graves Simcoe*, Vol. 1, 166.
28. Colonel E.A. Cruikshank, "Notes on the History of the District of Niagara, 1791–1793," Pamphlet #26 (1913?), 12, published by the Niagara Historical Society.
29. Innis, *Mrs. Simcoe's Diary*, 71.
30. The *Onondaga* was the same ship that had carried Lieutenant Governor and Mrs. Simcoe to Niagara from Kingston one month earlier.
31. Cruikshank, ed., *The Correspondence of Lieut. Governor John Graves Simcoe*, Vol. 1, 615–16.
32. *Ibid.*, 120.
33. Cruikshank, "Notes on the History of the District of Niagara, 1791–1793," 12.
34. Gow, "HRH Prince Edward, Duke of Kent: Father to Victoria," 134.
35. Cruikshank, ed., *The Correspondence of Lieut. Governor John Graves Simcoe*, Vol. 1, 205.
36. *Ibid.*
37. *Ibid.*, 173.
38. Innis, *Mrs. Simcoe's Diary*, 81.
39. Cruikshank, ed., *The Correspondence of Lieut. Governor John Graves Simcoe*, Vol. 1, 215.
40. Aspinall, *The Later Correspondence of George III*, Vol. 1, 618.
41. Gillen, *The Prince and His Lady*, 56.
42. Aspinall, *The Later Correspondence of George III*, Vol. 1, 618.

Chapter Five: Life In Lower Canada and War in the West Indies, 1792–1794

1. Egerton Ryerson, *The Loyalists of America and Their Times: From 1620 to 1816* (Toronto: William Briggs, 1880), 297–98.
2. During the final years of the eighteenth century, the Polish Diet, the governing body of Poland, was in a state of chaos, dominated by rival factions.
3. "The situation in France" refers to the French Revolution.
4. Gillen, *The Prince and His Lady*, 69–70.
5. Founded by Captain Joseph Quesnel de la Rivaudais (famous for having been arrested for trying to transport arms to the Americans during

the Revolution) in 1780, the Montreal theatre company was disbanded in 1817.

6. Serge Bernier, Jacques Castonguay *et al*, *Military History of Quebec City, 1608–2008* (Quebec City: Art Global, 2008), 207.

7. William James Anderson, *The Life of F.M., H.R.H. Edward, Duke of Kent, Illustrated by His Correspondence with the de Salaberry Family, never before published, extending from 1791 to 1814* (Toronto: Hunter, Rose and Company, 1870), 17.

8. *Ibid.*

9. *Ibid.*, 18.

10. *Ibid.*, 14.

11. The adjutant-general is responsible for developing the army's personnel policies and supporting its people.

12. Quoted in Mollie Gillen, *The Prince and His Lady*, 65.

13. Gillen, *The Prince and His Lady*, 63.

14. Anderson, *The Life of F.M., H.R.H. Edward, Duke of Kent*, 14–15.

15. Aspinall, *The Later Correspondence of George III, 1783–1793*, Vol. 2, 5–6.

16. *Ibid.*, 6.

17. As the representative of the King in Lower Canada, Alured Clarke alone was allowed to exercise the royal prerogative of pardoning a convicted and sentenced criminal.

18. Aspinall, *The Correspondence of George, Prince of Wales: 1770–1812*, Vol. 2, 258–59.

19. *Ibid.*, 20.

20. *Ibid.*, 344–45.

21. *Ibid.*, 375–77.

22. Sir Charles Grey, 1st Earl Grey, is the ancestor of Albert Henry George Grey, 4th Earl Grey and governor general of Canada (1904–11). For background on the correspondence, see A. Aspinall, *The Correspondence of George, Prince of Wales: 1770–1812*, Vol. 2, 392–93.

23. Aspinall, *The Later Correspondence of George III*, Vol. 2, 144.

24. *Ibid.*

25. John H. Graham, *Outlines of the History of Freemasonry in the Province of Quebec* (Quebec: John Lowell & Son, 1892), 27.

26. Jessica Harland-Jacobs, *Builders of Empire: Freemasons and British Imperialism: 1717–1927* (Chapel Hill: University of North Carolina Press, 2007), 133.

27. G. Norman Knight, "The Three Dukes of Kent," *The Masonic Record*, Vol. 46, No. 6 (1966): 163–64.

28. John Wilkes, *Encyclopaedia Londinensis*, Vol. XIV (London: J. Adlard, 1819), 490–97. The current grand master of the United Grand Lodge of England is His Royal Highness Prince Edward, Duke of Kent (b. 1935).

29. Edwin G. Burrows and Mike Wallace, *Gotham: A History of New York City to 1898* (New York: Oxford University Press, 1999), 286.

30. *Ibid.*, 314.

31. Royal Archives, Prince Edward to Prince of Wales, January 4, 1794. RA GEO/MAIN/45909-10.

32. Aspinall, *The Later Correspondence of George III*, Vol. 2, 184.

33. Quoted in Mollie Gillen, *The Prince and His Lady*, 82.

34. Anderson, *The Life of F.M., H.R.H. Edward, Duke of Kent*, 19.

35. *The Farmers' Library: Or, Vermont Political & Historical Register*, February 17, 1794, page 3.

36. It is interesting to note that a letter exists, dated June 10, 1792, between postmasters general Thomas de Grey, 2nd Baron Walsingham, and Philip Stanhope, 5th Earl of Chesterfield, regarding the bad state of repair of the packet ship *Roebuck*. Grey requested the hiring of two packet ships so that a mail service could be continued.

37. Samuel Adams Drake, *Historic Mansions and Highways Around Boston being of "Old Landmarks and Historical Fields of Middlesex,"* (Boston: Little, Brown and Company, 1899), 349–50.

38. Quoted in Heather S. Nathans, *Early American Theatre from the Revolution to Thomas Jefferson: Into the Hands of the People* (New York: Cambridge University Press, 2003), 79–80.

39. Quoted in Mollie Gillen, *A Prince and His Lady*, 85.

40. Aspinall, *The Later Correspondence of George III*, Vol. 2, 184.

41. The First French Republic was declared on September 22, 1792, and would last until it was replaced by the First Empire under Napoleon I on May 18, 1804.

42. Aspinall, *The Later Correspondence of George III*, Vol. 2, 188.

43. Of the three islands conquered by forces that included Prince Edward, Martinique and Guadeloupe remain part of France today. Her Majesty, Queen Elizabeth II, remains Queen of the independent realm of St. Lucia.

44. Aspinall, *The Later Correspondence of George III*, Vol. 2, 197–98.

45. *Ibid.*, 197–98.

Chapter Six: Edward's Golden Age of Halifax, 1794–1800

1. Thomas H. Raddall, *Halifax: Warden of the North*, (Halifax: Nimbus Classics, 2010), 110.

2. *Ibid.*

3. Another 15,000 Loyalists went to New Brunswick. Both St. John's Island (Prince Edward Island) and Cape Breton Island received 1,000 American settlers.

4. Rather than be called "Lieutenant Governor," John Wentworth continued to be called "Governor" as he had been in New Hampshire. The tradition

of calling the vice-regal representative of the Sovereign "Governor" continues in Nova Scotia today.

5. Nova Scotia Archives, John Wentworth to John King, May 19, 1794, #C0217/36.

6. *Ibid.*

7. *Ibid.*

8. Susan Burgess Shenstone, *So Obstinately Loyal: James Moody, 1744–1809* (Montreal: McGill-Queen's University Press, 2000), 232.

9. Founded by Lieutenant Governor John Wentworth five days after the declaration of war by France on February 3, 1793, the Nova Scotia Regiment was a provincial regiment under the jurisdiction of the commander-in-chief, and with Wentworth as its colonel. In 1794, the regiment was granted the honour of adding "Royal" to its name.

10. For more information on James Moody (born in New Jersey in 1744, died in Sissiboo, Nova Scotia, in 1809), see *Dictionary of Canadian Biography Online*.

11. Anderson, *The Life of F.M., H.R.H. Edward, Duke of Kent*, 23–24.

12. A coadjutor is a bishop appointed to assist a diocesan bishop, and is often also designated as his successor.

13. Anderson, *The Life of F.M., H.R.H. Edward, Duke of Kent*, 24.

14. Quoted in Mollie Gillen, "The Residences of the Duke of Kent," *History Today*, Vol. 11 (December 1971): 2–3.

15. James D. Kornwolf, *Architecture and Town Planning in Colonial North America*, Vol. III (Baltimore: The Johns Hopkins University Press, 2002), 1346.

16. Ian Walter Radforth, *Royal Spectacle: The 1860 Visit of the Prince of Wales to Canada and the United States* (Toronto: University of Toronto Press, 2004), 308.

17. Today, local residents have adopted the name Rockingham, in memory of the exclusive "Rockingham Club," to identify the estate that once existed there.

18. Thomas H. Raddall writes that the Rockingham Club comprised Sir John Wentworth, "the members of His Majesty's Council, the admiral, the commander of the garrison, several well-connected army and navy officers, and a number of Halifax gentry." Raddall, *Halifax: Warden of the North*, 132.

19. University of New Brunswick, Prince Edward to Henry Dundas, November 11, 1794. Loyalist Collection, Harriet Irving Library, MIC-Loyalist FC LMR .G7W3A4I6.

20. The Maroon Wars (1655–1739 and 1795–96) raged between the British colonial government of Jamaica and the descendants of the African slaves, who fled into the Cockpit Country in the interior of Jamaica after Oliver Cromwell's forces took control of the island in 1655.

21. John N. Grant, *The Maroons in Nova Scotia* (Halifax: Formac, 2002), 34.
22. Quoted in Grant, *The Maroons in Nova Scotia*, 36.
23. The uniform of a Maroon was distinguished by having white buttons marked with an insignia of an alligator holding a wheat sheaf, an olive branch, and inscribed "Jamaica to the Maroons 1796."
24. Of Halifax's five Martello Towers, only the Prince of Wales Tower still stands at the centre of Point Pleasant Park in Halifax. It was declared a National Historic Site in 1943 and fully restored in 1967.
25. Quoted in Paul David Nelson, *General Sir Guy Carleton, Lord Dorchester* (London: Associated Press, 2000), 233.
26. Aspinall, *Correspondence of George, Prince of Wales, 1770–1812*, Vol. III, 21–22.
27. *Ibid.*, 21–22.
28. Nova Scotia Archives, Prince Edward to Major-General Edmonston, December 27, 1795, 2002-045/009 #12.
29. "consequently it will be necessary to wait till the absolute retirement of my Lord [Dorchester], before I can judge *if it is to be my destiny to be one day Governor General of British North America,* or not." Dr. William James Anderson, *The Life of F.M., H.R.H. Edward, Duke of Kent, Illustrated by his correspondence with the de Salaberry family, never before published, extending from 1791 to 1814*, 35.
30. Anderson, *The Life of F.M., H.R.H. Edward, Duke of Kent*, 39.
31. Nova Scotia Archives, Prince Edward to William Edmeston, August 15, 1796, 2002-045/009.
32. *Ibid.*
33. Nova Scotia Archives, John Wentworth to John King, April 25, 1797, MG II, N.S. "A", Vol. A125.1997.C.O.217/37.
34. University of New Brunswick, Harriet Irving Library, William Waldegrave to Prince Edward, August 14, 1797, Loyalist Collection, MIC-Loyalist FC LMR .G7W3A4I6, Vol. 16.
35. *Ibid.*
36. University of New Brunswick, Harriet Irving Library, Prince Edward to William Waldegrave, August 26th, 1797, Loyalist Collection, MIC-Loyalist FC-LMR.G7W3A4I6, Vol. 16.
37. *Ibid.*
38. *Ibid.*
39. Aspinall, *The Later Correspondence of George III*, Vol. 3, 49–51.
40. The members of the committee were comprised of members of the Executive Council (Henry Newton, John Halliburton, and Benning Wentworth) and the House of Assembly (William Cochran, Lawrence Hartshorne, John George Pyke, Richard John Uniacke, and Michael Wallace).
41. Nova Scotia Archives, Address of the Lieutenant Governor, Council and

House of Assembly to H.R.H. Prince Edward, 1798, RG 5 Series A, Vol. 6, No. 91.

42. Nova Scotia Archives, Prince Edward's answer to address of the legislature, July 7, 1798, RG 1, Vol. 302 No. 68.

43. Brig.-Gen. E.A. Cruikshank and A.F. Hunter, *The Correspondence of The Honourable Peter Russell with Allied Documents Relating to His Administration of the Government of Upper Canada During the Official Term of Lieut.-Governor J.G. Simcoe While on a Leave of Absence* (Toronto: Ontario Historical Society, 1935), 274.

44. In 1780, the assembly of the Island of St. John had petitioned to change its name to "New Ireland," but their request was vetoed by the governor, Walter Patterson.

45. Anderson, *The Life of F. M., H.R.H. Edward, Duke of Kent*, 56.

46. Nova Scotia Archives, Duke of Kent to Henry Dundas, September 20, 1799, 2002-045/010 #1. Edward's efforts to reduce his debts were immediately hampered when his extensive library, comprising nearly 5,000 volumes, was lost at sea when the ship carrying it was shipwrecked off the coast of Sable Island that year. These books would need to be replaced.

47. For more information about the German congregation at St. George's Round Church, see the website at *www.roundchurch.ca*.

48. Nova Scotia Archives, Duke of Kent to Duke of Portland, November 21, 1799, MG II, N.S. "A," Vol. A130. C.O.217/71.

49. Louis Philippe, *Biographical Memoirs of Louis Philippe the First, Ex-king of the French* (London: Cradock & Co, 1848), 27.

50. Quoted in Mollie Gillen, *The Prince and His Lady*, 128.

51. A. Aspinall, *Correspondence of George, Prince of Wales, 1770–1812*, Vol. IV (London: Cassell, 1963), 121.

52. Aspinall, *Correspondence of George, Prince of Wales, 1770–1812*, 121–30.

53. Aspinall, *The Later Correspondence of George III*, Vol. 3, 352.

54. Nova Scotia Archives, Sir John Wentworth to John King, August 6, 1800, CO 217/37.

Chapter Seven: After Canada and Nova Scotia, 1800–1820

1. Nova Scotia Archives, John Graves Simcoe to the Duke of Kent, November 24, 1801, 2002-045/009 #20.

2. *Ibid.*, Duke of Kent to John Graves Simcoe, December 13, 1801, 2002-045/009 #20.

3. Mollie Gillen, *The Prince and His Lady*, 142.

4. Quoted in Mollie Gillen, *The Prince and His Lady*, 144.

5. Gillen, *The Prince and His Lady*, 143.

6. The Gibraltar mutiny is discussed in great detail by Mollie Gillen, *The Prince and His Lady*, 149–52.

7. Quoted in Mollie Gillen, *The Prince and His Lady*, 158–59.

8. Aspinall, *Correspondence of George, Prince of Wales, 1770–1812*, Vol. IV, 412.

9. Aspinall, *Correspondence of George, Prince of Wales, 1770–1812*, Vol. V, 106–07.

10. The Royal Archives was able to provide the following list of charities patronized by the Duke of Kent in 1819 (no official list exists): Patron of the Benevolent Society of St Patrick; Patron of the Society for the Relief of Widows and Orphans of Medical Men; Patron of the Clerkenwell General Philanthropic Society; Patron of the Friendly Female Society; Patron of St. Anne's Society Schools; Vice-patron of the City of London School of Instruction and Industry; President of The Corporation of the Caledonian Asylum; *Vice-Patron of the Royal Westminster Infirmary for Diseases of the Eye; President of the Infirmary for Asthma, Consumption and Other Diseases of the Lungs; President of the Lying-in Charity; Patron of the Eastern Dispensary; Vice-Patron of the City Dispensary; Patron of the City of London Truss-Society for the Relief of the Ruptured Poor; and Patron of the National Benevolent Institution.*

11. Spencer Perceval, *The royal or delicate investigation into the conduct of Her Royal Highness, the Princess of Wales : before Lords Erskine, Spencer, Grenville, and Ellenborough, the four special commissioners of inquiry, appointed by His Majesty in the year 1806. Containing the depositions of all the evidences, copies of the various letters, statements, narratives, reports, and minutes of council, &c. &c.* (London: C. Chapple, 1806).

12. Aspinall, *Correspondence of George, Prince of Wales, 1770–1812*, Vol. VI, 26.

13. Anderson, *The Life of F.M., H.R.H. Edward, Duke of Kent*, 118.

14. *Ibid.*, 135.

15. *Ibid.*, 134.

16. *Ibid.*, 136–37.

17. Quoted in F. Murray Greenwood, *Legacies of Fear: Law and Politics in Quebec in the Era of the French Revolution* (Toronto: The Osgoode Society, 1993), 321.

18. Anderson, *The Life of F.M., H.R.H. Edward, Duke of Kent*, 171.

19. Aspinall, *Correspondence of George, Prince of Wales, 1770–1812*, Vol. VII, 276–77.

20. *Ibid.*, 292–93.

21. *Ibid.*, 294–95.

22. Anderson, *The Life of F.M., H.R.H. Edward, Duke of Kent*, 208.

23. It is worth noting that the Canadian Voltigeurs fell under the Lower Canada Militia Act, and were not part of the British Army. By making the regiment provincial in nature, Governor General Prevost ensured that Roman Catholics could serve as officers (Catholics were banned from being officers in the British Army) and that the men serving in the corps

could be not be flogged.

24. Anderson, *The Life of F.M., H.R.H. Edward, Duke of Kent*, 210–11.

25. *Ibid.*, 213.

26. *Ibid.*, 214.

27. It is interesting that while Charles de Salaberry was created a companion of the Order of the Bath, Isaac Brock had been created a knight (a higher level within the order) three days before his death.

28. During my final days of working on this book I received a fascinating note from Eleanor Sewell Russell: "Jonathan Sewell and Edward, the future Duke of Kent, were well known to each other in 1793 when the Duke resided in Quebec City for over a year. Edward had brought his military band with him from England and enjoyed music of all kinds as did Jonathan. In 1794, according to the Baptismal register, Jonathan sired a son out of wedlock. However, even today, many believe that the baby was in fact born to the Duke's mistress, Mme Julie de St. Laurent, and Jonathan agreed to adopt the boy. This boy, John St. Alban Sewell, is my great, great grandfather." Eleanor's husband, constitutional scholar Peter Russell, later commented to me that he had "married a princess."

29. Dictionary of the Canadian Biography Online, 1836-1850 (Vol. VII). *www.biographi.ca/009004-119.01-e.php?id_nbr=3655.*

30. Jonathan Sewell and John Beverley Robinson, *Plan for a General Legislative Union of the British Provinces in North America* (London: W. Clowes, 1814), 7.

31. Sewell and Robinson, *Plan for a General Legislative Union of the British Provinces,* 11.

32. Royal Archives, Duke of Kent to Jonathan Sewell, November 30, 1814. RA-GEO/ADD21/30.

33. Sir C.P. Lucas, ed., *Report on the Affairs of British North American*, Vol. II (Oxford: Clarendon Press, 1912), 320.

34. Quoted in Donald Grant Creighton, *John A. MacDonald: The Young Politician, the Old Chieftain* (Toronto: Macmillan, 1998), 207.

35. Canada is unique in the Commonwealth for still celebrating the birthday of Queen Victoria. "Victoria Day" not only recognizes the birth of the Queen under which Confederation occurred, but also serves as Canada's official celebration of the current Sovereign's birthday.

36. Stanley Weintraub, *Victoria*, (New York: Dutton, 1987), 42–48.

37. Fraser, *The Lives of the Kings and Queens of England*, 293.

38. *Ibid.*, 285–95.

39. Queen Victoria, Personal Diary (Princess Beatrice's Copies), February 27 and May 22, 1867. © Her Majesty Queen Elizabeth II, *www.queenvictori-asjournals.org.*

40. Prince Edward Island is known today as "The Cradle of Confederation."

Selected Bibliography

ARCHIVES

Archives Ontario
Library and Archives Canada
Nova Scotia Archives
Gow, Jean Donald. *HRH Prince Edward, Duke of Kent: Father to Victoria.* Halifax, 1991. Nova Scotia Archives (2002-045/006 2).
Royal Archives, Windsor Castle
University of New Brunswick, Harriet Irving Library, The Loyalist Collection

ARTICLES

Cruikshank, Colonel E.A. "Notes on the History of the District of Niagara, 1791–1793." Pamphlet #26 (1913?). Published by the Niagara Historical Society.
Gillen, Mollie. "The Residences of the Duke of Kent." *History Today.* Vol. 11 (December 1971): 1–6.
Golder, Frank A. "Catherine II. and The American Revolution." *The American Historical Review.* Vol. 21, No. 1 (1915): 92–96.
Knight, G. Norman. "The Three Dukes of Kent." *The Masonic Record.* Vol. 46, No. 6, 1966.

McNab, David T. "The Promise That He Gave To My Grand Father Was Very Sweet: The Gun Shot Treaty of 1792 at the Bay of Quinte." *The Canadian Journal of Native Studies.* Vol. XVI, No. 2 (1996): 293–314.

BOOKS

Primary Sources

Anderson, Dr. William James. *The Life of F.M., H.R.H. Edward, Duke of Kent, Illustrated by his correspondence with the de Salaberry family, never before published, extending from 1791 to 1814.* Toronto: Hunter, Rose & Company, 1870.

Aspinall, A. *The Correspondence of George, Prince of Wales: 1770–1812,* Vol. 1–8. London: Cassell & Company, 1964.

———. *The Later Correspondence of George III, 1783–1793, Vol. 1–6.* Cambridge: University Press, 1962.

Corbin, Ingrim. *Georgina; or, Anecdotes of George the Third. With a selection of Poetical Effusions and other Eulugiums on His Character, and on that of H.R.H. The Duke of Kent.* London: W. Whitmore, Paternoster Row, 1820.

Cornwell, B. *A description of Gibraltar: with an account of the blockade, siege, the Attempt by Nine sail of Fire-Ships, the Sally made from the Garrison, and every Thing remarkable or worthy Notice that has occurred in that Place since the Commencement of the Spanish War: Likewise The vast importance of this valuable Fortress to Great Britain clearly stated and explained.* London: Richardson and Urquhart, 1782.

Cruikshank, Brigadier General E.A., ed. *The Correspondence of Lieut. Governor John Graves Simcoe, with allied documents relating to his administration of the government of Upper Canada,* Vol. 1–6. Toronto: The Ontario Historical Society, 1923.

———. and A.F. Hunter, eds. *The Correspondence of The Honourable Peter Russell with Allied Documents Relating to His Administration of the Government of Upper Canada During the Official Term of Lieut.-Governor J.G. Simcoe While on a Leave of Absence.* Toronto: Ontario Historical Society, 1935.

Drake, Samuel Adams. *Historic Mansions and Highways Around Boston being of "Old Landmarks and Historical Fields of Middlesex."* Boston: Little, Brown and Company, 1899.

Fortescue, Sir John, ed. *The Correspondence of King George the Third from 1760 to December 1783, printed from the original papers in the Royal Archives at Windsor Castle.* London: Macmillan and Co., 1927.

Graham, John. *Outlines of the History of Freemasonry in the Province of Quebec.* Quebec: John Lowell & Son, 1892.

Hamilton, Sir Richard Vesey, ed. *Letters and papers of Admiral of the fleet Sir*

Thos. Byam Martin, G.C.B. London: Navy Records Society, 1898.

Morgan, Henry James. *The Dominion annual register and review for the thirteenth year of the Canadian union, 1879.* Ottawa: Maclean, Roger & Co., 1880.

Perceval, Spencer. *The royal or delicate investigation into the conduct of Her Royal Highness, the Princess of Wales : before Lords Erskine, Spencer, Grenville, and Ellenborough, the four special commissioners of inquiry, appointed by His Majesty in the year 1806. Containing the depositions of all the evidences, copies of the various letters, statements, narratives, reports, and minutes of council, &c. &c.* London: C. Chapple, 1806.

Philippe, Louis. *Biographical memoirs of Louis Philippe the first, ex-King of the French.* London: Cradock & Co, 1848.

Rose, George Maclean. *A Cyclopedia of Canadian Men & Women: Being Chiefly Men of the Time.* Toronto: Rose Publishing, 1886.

Ryerson, Egerton. *The Loyalists of America and Their Times: From 1620 to 1816.* Toronto: William Briggs, 1880.

Scadding, Henry. *Letter to Sir Joseph Banks, (president of the Royal Society of Great Britain) written by Lieut.-Governor Simcoe, in 1791, prior to his departure from England for the purpose of organizing the new province of Upper Canada; to which is added the five official speeches delivered by him at the opening or closing of Parliament in the same province.* Toronto: Copp Clark, 1890.

Sewell, Jonathan. *Plan for a General Legislative Union of the British Provinces in North America.* London: W. Cowes, 1824.

The London Gazette. London: H.M. Stationery Off. (No. 10777), October 31–November 1, 1767.

The London Gazette. London: H.M. Stationery Off. (No. 10785), November 28–December 1, 1767.

Watkins, John. *A Biographical Memoir of His Late Royal Highness Frederick, Duke of York and Albany; Commander-In-Chief of the Forces of Great Britain, etc., etc.* London: Henry Fisher, Son, and Co., 1827.

Wetherall, Major Joseph. *An Historical Account of His Majesty's First, or Royal Regiment of Foot.* London: W. Clowes, 1832.

Wheater, W. *Historical Record of The Seventh or Royal Regiment of Fusiliers.* Leeds: 1875.

Wilkes, John. *Encyclopaedia Londinensis.* Vol. XIV. London: J. Adlard, 1819.

Williamson, John. *The Elements of Military Arrangement, and of the Discipline of War; adapted to the practice of the British infantry,* Vol. 1–2. London: Medicine, Science and Technology, 1791.

Secondary Sources

Beacock Fryer, Mary and Christopher Dracott. *John Graves Simcoe, 1752–1806: A Biography*. Toronto: Dundurn Press, 1998.

Bernier, Serge, Jacques Castonguay, *et al. Military History of Quebec City: 1608–2008*. Quebec City: Art Global, 2008.

Biggar, Henry Percival, ed. *The Voyages of Jacques Cartier*. Toronto: University of Toronto Press, 1993.

Bousfield, Arthur, and Garry Toffoli. *Home to Canada: Royal Tours, 1786–2010*. Toronto: Dundurn Press, 2010.

Buckley, Roger Norman. *The British Army in the West Indies: Society and the Military in the Revolutionary Age*. Gainesville, FL: University Press of Florida, 1998.

Burrows, Edwin G., and Mike Wallace. *Gotham: A History of New York City to 1898*. New York: Oxford University Press, 1999.

Butler, Nancy, Richard D. Merritt, and Michael Power. *The Capital Years: Niagara-On-The-Lake 1792–1796*. Toronto: Dundurn Press, 1996.

Byers, Mary, and Margaret McBurney. *Atlantic Hearth*. Toronto: University of Toronto Press, 1994.

Cameron, Christina. *Charles Baillairgé: Architect and Engineer*. Toronto: McGill-Queen's University Press, 1989.

Catanzariti, John, ed. *The Papers of Thomas Jefferson*. Princeton: Princeton University Press, 1990.

Charlot, Monica. *Victoria: The Young Queen*. Cambridge: Blackwell, 1991.

Conrad, Margaret, and Alvin Finkel. *History of the Canadian Peoples: Beginnings to 1867*. Toronto: Addison Wesley Longman, 2002.

Creighton, Donald Grant. *John A. Macdonald: The Young Politician, the Old Chieftain*. Toronto: Macmillan, 1998.

Cuthbertson, Brian C. *The Loyalist Governor*. Halifax: Petheric Press, 1983.

Eaton, Arthur Wentworth Hamilton. *Chapters in the History of Halifax, Nova Scotia: Rhode Island Settlers in Hants County, Nova Scotia: Alexander McNutt the Colonizer.* n.p., 1913–1919.

Fischer, David Hackett. *Champlain's Dream*. Toronto: Vintage, 2009.

Francis, R. Douglas, Richard Jones, and Donald B. Smith. *Origins: Canadian History to Confederation, Sixth Edition*. Toronto: Nelson, 2009.

Fraser, Antonia, ed. *The Lives of the Kings and Queens of England*. London: Phoenix Illustrated, 1997.

Fulford, Roger. *Royal Dukes*. London: Collins, 1973.

Gill, Gillian. *We Two: Victoria and Albert: Rulers, Partners, Rivals*. New York: Random House, 2009.

Gillen, Mollie. *The Prince and His Lady*. London: Sidgwick & Jackson, 1970.

Grant, John H. *The Maroons in Nova Scotia*. Halifax: Formac Publishing

Company, 2002.

Greenwood, F. Murray. *Legacies of Fear: Law and Politics in Quebec in the Era of the French Revolution.* Toronto: The Osgoode Society, 1993.

Hall, Roger, and S.W. Shelton. *"The Rising Country": The Hale-Amherst Correspondence, 1799–1825.* Toronto: The Champlain Society, 2002.

Harland-Jacobs, Jessica. *Builders of Empire: Freemasons and British Imperialism: 1717–1927.* Chapel Hill, NC: University of North Carolina Press, 2007.

Harris, Richard Colebrook. *The Seigneurial System in Early Canada: A Geographical Study.* Montreal: McGill-Queen's University Press, 1984.

Innis, Mary Quayle, ed. *Mrs. Simcoe's Diary.* Toronto: Macmillan, 1978.

Kelleher, J.P. *The Royal Fusiliers: The City of London Regiment.* London: City of London Headquarters RRF, [1993?].

———. *The 7th Royal Fusiliers and their Part in The American War of Independence 1775–1781 and New Orleans 1815.* London: The Fusilier Museum London, 2008.

Kelsay, Isabel Thompson. *Joseph Brant, 1743–1807: Man of Two Worlds.* Syracuse, NY: Syracuse University Press, 1984.

Kornwolf, James D. *Architecture and Town Planning in Colonial North America,* Vol. III. Baltimore, MD: The Johns Hopkins University Press, 2002.

Nathans, Heather S. *Early American Theatre from the Revolution to Thomas Jefferson: Into the Hands of the People.* New York: Cambridge University Press, 2003.

National Parks Branch, Canada. *The Halifax Citadel.* Ottawa: Ministry of Northern Affairs and Natural Resources, [1957?].

Nelson, Paul David. *General Sir Guy Carleton, Lord Dorchester: Soldier-Statesman of Early British Canada.* Madison: Fairleigh Dickinson University Presses, 2000.

Pacey, Elizabeth. *Georgian Halifax.* Hantsport: Lancelot Press, 1987.

Porter, McKenzie. *Overture to Victoria.* London: Alvin Redman, 1962.

Pound, Richard W., ed. *Fitzhenry and Whiteside Book of Canadian Facts and Dates.* Toronto: Fitzhenry & Whiteside, 2005.

Prochaska, Frank. *The Eagle & The Crown: Americans and the British Monarchy.* New Haven: Yale University Press, 2008.

Raddall, Thomas H. *Halifax: Warden of the North.* Halifax: Nimbus Publishing Ltd., 2010.

Radforth, Ian Walter. *Royal Spectacle: The 1860 Visit of the Prince Of Wales to Canada and the United States.* Toronto: University of Toronto Press, 2004.

Raugh, Harold E. *The Victorians at War, 1815–1914: An Encyclopedia of British Military History.* Santa Barbara, CA: ABC-CLIO Inc., 2004.

Rhodehamel, John, ed. *George Washington, Writings.* New York: The Library of America, 1997.

Shenstone, Susan Burgess. *So Obstinately Loyal: James Moody, 1744–1809.*

Montreal: McGill-Queen's University Press, 2000.

Sutcliffe, Sheila. *Martello Towers*. Cranbury, DE: Associated University Presses Inc., 1972.

Syrett, Harold A., ed. *The Papers of Alexander Hamilton*. New York: Columbia University Press, 1966.

The Sault de montmorency. Quebéc: Société des établissements de plein air du Québec, 1993.

Thomas, Earl. *Sir John Johnson: Loyalist Baronet*. Toronto: Dundurn Press, 1986.

Tupper, Ferdinand Brock. *The Life and Correspondence of Sir Isaac Brock, K.B.* Toronto: Canadiana House, 1981.

Twohig, Dorothy. *The Journal of the Proceedings of the President, 1793–1797*. Charlottesville, VA: University Press of Virginia, 1981.

Weintraub, Stanley. *Victoria: An Intimate Biography*. New York: Truman Talley Books, 1987.

Woodham-Smith, Cecil. *Queen Victoria: Her Life and Times, 1819–1861*. Vol. I. London: Hamish Hamilton, 1972.

Young, A.H. *The Parish Registry of Kingston Upper Canada, 1785–1811*. Kingston: British Whig Publishing Company, 1921.

Zinn, Howard. *A People's History of the United States*. New York: Harper, 2003.

WEBSITES

Christ Church, Sorel: *www.christchurchsorel.ca*

College of St. George, Windsor Castle: *www.stgeorges-windsor.org*

Dictionary of Canadian Biography Online: *www.biographi.ca*

"King George III: Mad or Misunderstood?," BBC News, 13 July 2004: *www.bbc.com*

Moran, Donald M. "George Washington's Generals: Major-General Richard Montgomery." *Liberty Tree Magazine* (2006): *www.revolutionarywararchives.org*

Queen Victoria's Journals: *www.queenvictoriasjournals.org*

St. George's Round Church: *www.roundchurch.ca*

Index